AVOIDANT

*How to Love
(or Leave)
a Dismissive Partner*

JEB KINNISON

Library of Congress Control Number: 2014953024

Cover photo: Shutterstock

AVOIDANT

*How to Love
(or Leave)
a Dismissive Partner*

JEB KINNISON

Contents

Author's Note

This book is about finding a way to be happy individually and as a couple when either or both have avoidant attachment issues—either dismissive or fearful-avoidant (which is sometimes called anxious-avoidant.)

Not knowing anything about attachment types, many people discover their partner is avoidant only after a few years of distress, and by accident when someone tells them about attachment types, or they do some research online. Having an avoidant attachment type is not a disease or disorder; it simply means early childhood experiences with caregivers left them with little trust for intimate companions, and a desire to avoid the pain that might come if they became dependent and then were hurt by a loved one's failure to help them, as likely happened to them when they were infants. This subconscious lack of trust and desire for intimacy means they are "intimacy avoidant"— note that this is unrelated to Avoidant Personality Disorder, a confusing name for a DSM-IV-TR-defined disorder of oversensitivity and social anxiety leading to isolation.

If your partner is avoidant, you will recognize the signs immediately in reading the chapters on Dismissive-Avoidants and Fearful-Avoidants. Some of the turmoil their relationships undergo is centered around their inability and lack of desire to respond supportively to request signals from their partner; the disappointment and anger of the partner then feeds back into further withdrawal by the dismissive, and the relationship begins to crack under the strain.

One of the points of this book is that not only can avoidants change (with therapy and motivation) to be more supportive, but their partners can learn to understand and accept more their need for emotional distance. Your avoidant partner is a complex individual with a history and many characteristics beyond attachment type; while some avoidants (especially the dismissive variety) are likely to be tough to live with for almost anyone, yours may be able to modify their thoughts and behavior enough to improve your relationship. And you may find more happiness by understanding better how they feel.

Preface

My previous book on attachment types (*Bad Boyfriends: Using Attachment Theory to Avoid Mr. (or Ms.) Wrong and Make You a Better Partner*) and the accompanying web site (JebKinnison.com) put me in contact with a lot of readers and suggested there is great interest in the narrower topic of how to improve existing relationships with people who are Avoidant[1]—either Dismissive-Avoidant or more rarely, Fearful-Avoidant. I wrote the first book for an audience still seeking a good partner, with the primary goal of telling the unattached what to look out for to find the best partner for them. But there are many readers in troubled marriages now who are looking for help. There are also young people already invested in a relationship short of marriage who'd like help deciding if they should stick with it.

The reason why there is so much interest is the large number of people in relationships with Avoidants who struggle with their lack of responsiveness and inability to tolerate real intimacy. Relationships between an Avoidant and a partner of another attachment type are the largest group of unhappy relationships, and people who love their partners and who may have started families and had children with an Avoidant will work very hard to try to make their relationships work better, out of love for their partner and children as well as their own happiness. And it's also true that the Avoidants in these relationships are more than likely unhappy with the situation as well—retreating into their shells and feeling harassed for being asked to respond with positive feeling when they have little to give.

The other reason why so many people are looking for help on this topic is that it is an almost impossible problem. Couples counsellors rarely have the time or knowledge to work with an Avoidant and will often advise the spouse to give up on a Dismissive, especially, whose lack of responsiveness looks like cruelty or contempt (and sometimes it is!) Yet there is some hope—though it may take years and require educating the Avoidant on the patterns of good couples communication, if both partners want to change their patterns toward more secure and satisfying models, it can be done.

Individual therapy for the motivated Avoidant can move their default attachment style toward Secure, and to the extent that problems have been made worse by an overly clingy and demanding Anxious-Preoccupied partner, therapy can help there, as well. Insecure partners who read and absorb the lessons of these books will have a head start on noticing and restraining themselves when they are slipping into an unsatisfying communications pattern, and an intellectual understanding of the bad patterns is a step toward unlearning them.

I'm not going to promise anyone that their difficult Avoidant can be reformed; that depends on both partners, the depth of their problems, and their motivation and ability to change over time. But many difficult marriages and relationships can be greatly improved, and the people in them can learn to be happier, with even modest improvements in understanding how they can best communicate support for each other.

For those reading who have not read my previous book or are less familiar with attachment types, I've included a beefed-up section on attachment theory and attachment types from *Bad Boyfriends*. Feel free to skip to Avoidants in Relationships if you have already read *Bad Boyfriends* and don't need a review.

Regular readers of JebKinnison.com will notice I have included edited versions of some material previously posted there. Also, the accounts of real relationships have had names and details changed for privacy.

Note I have adopted a mixed treatment of pronouns; sometimes making an unfortunate plural "their" stand in for "his or her," sometimes using one sex or the other as seems reasonable. Similarly, I capitalize the attachment types ("Dismissive") when I am referring to a person of that type, but not when I need to use the terms many times.

I'd like to especially thank Profs. Phillip Shaver and Mario Mikulincer, the authors of *Attachment in Adulthood: Structure, Dynamics, and Change*, which was wonderfully helpful in summarizing the research into many topics in the field. I would have been unable to get access to many of the studies they cite, and their broad overview of each topic was invaluable.

— Jeb Kinnison

Part One

Couples Communication

Chapter 1

People Who Need People

Our culture is full of stories about love and relationships. First there's the "fairy tale" of two lovers finding their uniquely perfect partner, falling madly and mutually "in love" (before they can possibly really know each other), and living happily ever after in a cottage with a white picket fence. While this does happen, it's not common, and real tales of love and long-term partnership are rarely so simple and sweet. Then there's the recent hubbub over "codependence"—an idea which began in addiction studies, where an alcoholic, drug addict, or other self-destructive person is enabled by a partner who works to prevent the addict from either getting better or reaching the point of despair sufficient to convince the addict to start anew. Is dependence on another a bad thing, or unhealthy as sometimes implied? No, of course not—we are all dependent as children, and depend on each other more or less our entire lives to accomplish things and feel happy. Being able to depend on a reliable person when you need it is good. Being unable to function when you need to without the support of others is bad. The most secure children are raised by mothers who seem to sense it almost before their child needs help and assist immediately and just enough, while not hovering or invading the child's independence when they are exploring the world just fine alone. We see that the same "just when needed, just the right amount" principle of dependence acts between the best partners, and best friends. The best partner is responsive to your signals, and you as a good partner signal only when you really need help. Most of the trouble in relationships is about bad signaling and poor responses.

Chapter 2

Touch and Response

The basics of affect regulation (the patterns of signals between people which regulate the feelings they have for each other) were set forth by Mikulincer, Shaver, and Pereg[2]. It is both obvious and profound: it seems so simple as to not be worth describing, and yet underlying almost all our emotional signals to each other is one of these basic templates. Recognize these and you will understand why intentionally holding back on a response is alienating, why constant messages asking for reassurance can drive even the most patient partner away, and how we unconsciously "manage" our relationships by drawing others closer or pushing them away using these patterns. The simplest view is that a partner who is anxious sends a message to the other asking "Are you there?", and either gets a response "I am here for you" and is thus reassured, or gets no response or a negative response, and thus grows more anxious.

There are three basic strategies discussed in this section:[3]

- Security-based strategy
- Hyperactivation, or Anxiety-Attachment strategy
- Attachment-avoidance strategy

The flowchart for the **security-based** strategy:

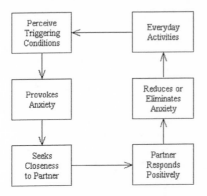

One partner's anxiety is triggered by external problems or simply a lack of recent reassurance. He or she signals (by moving closer, or asking for reassurance, or sending a message) the other partner, who responds with a message of reassurance (by snuggling closer, or saying something supportive, or sending a positive message back). Reassured, life goes on for both of them and anxiety-producing threats are dealt with.

The flowchart for **hyperactivation**, or the anxiety-attachment strategy:

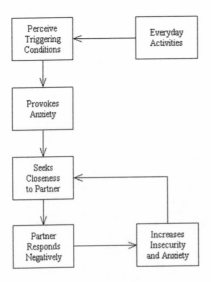

Here the partner asking for help or assurance gets either no response or a negative response—the other partner either fails to message back or sends a message refusing support. For example, the partner seeking assurance moves closer and tries for a hug, but the declining partner gets up and leaves. Or a direct statement asking for help ("I need you to go with me to the nursery so we can pick out some new plants") is met by rejection ("I don't have time to go with you since I have to pick up your brat after his soccer practice.") The response in this case increases anxiety and leads to more insistent messages asking for support; the requester is anxious and the decliner has even more reason to see themselves as put-upon by the requester's demands. If this cycle repeats too often, the attachment will weaken and the next strategy, attachment-avoidance, will be used.

This is flowchart for the **attachment-avoidance** strategy:

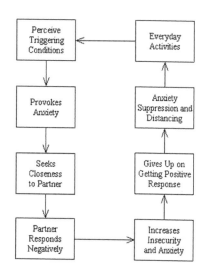

Here the partner requesting assurance handles rejection by *distancing* —lowering their expectations of support from the other partner. This pattern shows the breakdown of the request-assurance system and if predominant ultimately results in a broken or unhappy relationship. Note that nothing is inherently good or bad about any of these patterns, and all relationships have moments in the less secure loops -

but a couple which spends most of its time cycling through the hyperactivation or attachment-avoidance message cycles is not likely to feel happy and secure in their relationship.

Chapter 3

Best Practices for Couples

The Gottman Institute has been studying what makes for a happy marriage for many years, and their techniques and materials are widely used in couples counselling. *The Atlantic* had an excellent article (see link in footnote) by Emily Esfahani Smith which describes the studies they've undertaken and the results—which are very simple: couples who have happy marriages are responsive to and respectful of each other's requests for attention.

I described the basic request-response patterns in the previous section, "Touch and Response." The takeaway: the most important behavior an avoidant type can work on to increase the happiness of their relationships is to practice positive response even when their impulse is to deny response or respond negatively; and the most important behavior an anxious-preoccupied type can work on is to curb the impulse to request attention and reassurance when their partner is busy or irritated. In both cases, one needs to understand how it feels to be the other partner, and tune your request or response to their needs as well as your own. Cultivate the habit of considering your partner's state before responding carelessly or asking for reassurance, and the relationship is much more likely to reach a happy state of mutual trust and love.

> Every day in June, the most popular wedding month of the year, about 13,000 American couples will say "I do," committing to a lifelong relationship that will be full of friendship, joy, and love that will carry them forward to their final days on this earth.

Except, of course, it doesn't work out that way for most people. The majority of marriages fail, either ending in divorce and separation or devolving into bitterness and dysfunction. Of all the people who get married, only three in ten remain in healthy, happy marriages, as psychologist Ty Tashiro points out in his book *The Science of Happily Ever After,* which was published earlier this year.[*]

About half the population has an attachment type that tends to make a happy marriage more difficult to achieve. The Secure types, about 50% of the population, are more likely to marry each other and find this kind of supportive but unintrusive communication easier. The Dismissive-Avoidant and Fearful-Avoidant tend to be less supportive and reject true intimacy, and so see requests as clingy demands; while the Anxious-Preoccupied have an excessive need for reassurance that drives them to request attention more often and with less respect for their partner's state of mind.

From the data they gathered, Gottman separated the couples into two major groups: the masters and the disasters. The masters were still happily together after six years. The disasters had either broken up or were chronically unhappy in their marriages. When the researchers analyzed the data they gathered on the couples, they saw clear differences between the masters and disasters. The disasters looked calm during the interviews, but their physiology, measured by the electrodes, told a different story. Their heart rates were quick, their sweat glands were active, and their blood flow was fast. Following thousands of couples longitudinally, Gottman found that the more physiologically active the couples were in the lab, the quicker their relationships deteriorated over time.

But what does physiology have to do with anything? The problem was that the disasters showed all the signs of arousal—

of being in fight-or-flight mode—in their relationships. Having a conversation sitting next to their spouse was, to their bodies, like facing off with a saber-toothed tiger. Even when they were talking about pleasant or mundane facets of their relationships, they were prepared to attack and be attacked. This sent their heart rates soaring and made them more aggressive toward each other. For example, each member of a couple could be talking about how their days had gone, and a highly aroused husband might say to his wife, "Why don't you start talking about your day. It won't take you very long."

The masters, by contrast, showed low physiological arousal. They felt calm and connected together, which translated into warm and affectionate behavior, even when they fought. It's not that the masters had, by default, a better physiological make-up than the disasters; it's that masters had created a climate of trust and intimacy that made both of them more emotionally and thus physically comfortable.[5]

The positive health benefits of a happy marriage come from the reductions in stress and worry seen when one has a trusted and respected partner there to assist. An unhappy relationship with a partner who is adversarial and undermining is worse than no relationship at all.

The study revealed the request-response dynamics of the good relationships, which tended to reinforce trust and a sense of closeness, while the bad relationships showed carelessness in both requests and responses were damaging to the relationship and could predict divorce:

Throughout the day, partners would make requests for connection, what Gottman calls "bids." For example, say that the husband is a bird enthusiast and notices a goldfinch fly across the yard. He might say to his wife, "Look at that beautiful bird outside!" He's not just commenting on the bird here: he's requesting a response from his wife—a sign of interest or support—hoping they'll connect, however momentarily, over the bird.

The wife now has a choice. She can respond by either "turning toward" or "turning away" from her husband, as Gottman puts it. Though the bird-bid might seem minor and silly, it can actually reveal a lot about the health of the relationship. The husband thought the bird was important enough to bring it up in conversation and the question is whether his wife recognizes and respects that.

People who turned toward their partners in the study responded by engaging the bidder, showing interest and support in the bid. Those who didn't—those who turned away —would not respond or respond minimally and continue doing whatever they were doing, like watching TV or reading the paper. Sometimes they would respond with overt hostility, saying something like, "Stop interrupting me, I'm reading."

These bidding interactions had profound effects on marital well-being. Couples who had divorced after a six-year follow up had "turn-toward bids" 33 percent of the time. Only three in ten of their bids for emotional connection were met with intimacy. The couples who were still together after six years had "turn-toward bids" 87 percent of the time. Nine times out of ten, they were meeting their partner's emotional needs.

By observing these types of interactions, Gottman can predict with up to 94 percent certainty whether couples—straight or gay, rich or poor, childless or not—will be broken up, together and unhappy, or together and happy several years later. Much of it comes down to the spirit couples bring to the relationship. Do they bring kindness and generosity; or contempt, criticism, and hostility?⁶

The accumulated record of sensitivity to the other's needs either cements the bond or gradually erodes it. The habit of responding thoughtfully and positively even when interrupted or annoyed demonstrates love for the partner, while either not responding or responding negatively demonstrates contempt or indifference—this is commonly the Avoidant's tendency. Meanwhile, the Anxious-Preoccupied are focused on their own need for constant reassurance, and over-request regardless of their partner's state; this is as thoughtless in its way as the Avoidant's dismissal.

> Contempt, they have found, is the number one factor that tears couples apart. People who are focused on criticizing their partners miss a whopping 50 percent of positive things their partners are doing and they see negativity when it's not there. People who give their partner the cold shoulder—deliberately ignoring the partner or responding minimally—damage the relationship by making their partner feel worthless and invisible, as if they're not there, not valued. And people who treat their partners with contempt and criticize them not only kill the love in the relationship, but they also kill their partner's ability to fight off viruses and cancers. Being mean is the death knell of relationships.

> Kindness, on the other hand, glues couples together. Research independent from theirs has shown that kindness (along with emotional stability) is the most important predictor of satisfaction and stability in a marriage. Kindness makes each partner feel cared for, understood, and validated—feel loved. "My bounty is as boundless as the sea," says Shakespeare's Juliet. "My love as deep; the more I give to thee, / The more I have, for both are infinite." That's how kindness works too: there's a great deal of evidence showing the more someone receives or witnesses kindness, the more they will be kind themselves,

which leads to upward spirals of love and generosity in a relationship.

There are two ways to think about kindness. You can think about it as a fixed trait: either you have it or you don't. Or you could think of kindness as a muscle. In some people, that muscle is naturally stronger than in others, but it can grow stronger in everyone with exercise. Masters tend to think about kindness as a muscle. They know that they have to exercise it to keep it in shape. They know, in other words, that a good relationship requires sustained hard work.

"If your partner expresses a need," explained Julie Gottman, "and you are tired, stressed, or distracted, then the generous spirit comes in when a partner makes a bid, and you still turn toward your partner."[7]

In the chapter "Teaching Avoidants to Use Empathy," we'll discuss how studies have shown those who habitually don't feel much empathy can be trained to exercise it consciously. Similarly, in the chapter "Calming the Anxious-Preoccupied" we'll go into the Anxious-Preoccupied habit of over-requesting contact and confirmation, which tends to make even the Secure adopt an Avoidant style of negative response.

This advice is very simple—treat your partner like the most important person in the world to you, with the best manners you can muster. And even if you find it hard at first to habitually be kind when you are not feeling it, making the effort to fake it until it becomes a habit will pay enormous dividends in the happiness of your marriage, and the regard of everyone in your life as you treat them with more kindness and respect—because once you get in the habit, you will tend to treat everyone with more consideration.

Further reading:

Dr. John Gottman's book (*The Seven Principles for Making Marriage Work*) is a great guide on how to strive for secure attachment with your partner by open and positive communication combined with empathy.

Part Two

Attachment Types

Chapter 4

What are Attachment Types?

Psychologists have noticed that children whose caregivers (generally, mothers) were either unresponsive to their needs or overly concerned by their needs tended to have children with problems relating to others in a secure way.

- If the child's needs had been ignored or only grudgingly attended to, the child would be *avoidant*—meaning the child would stop seeking comfort, or ignore the caregiver.
- Children who are given a mix of comfort when needed and inattention or unwanted attention inconsistently often end up *anxious-preoccupied*—the child is afraid and needs constant reassurance to feel safe, often clinging to the caregiver and being too afraid to explore out of sight.
- A *secure* child, on the other hand, was used to having their cries met with comfort and assistance, but only when needed, and learned the language of love—messages of "I'm here if you need me," and "You're safe." Secure children eventually feel safe enough to explore and leave the caregiver's side without fear, since they know their cries will be heard and responded to even from a distance.

This field became known as *Attachment Theory*. In the late 80s, this understanding of children's attachment types was extended to adults. Early upbringing tends to set up the emotional mechanisms for handling all significant relationships, with an adult's style of handling partner and even friendship relationships heavily influenced by the patterns learned in early childhood. And adults with secure patterns have more satisfying, lasting, and successful relationships than adults with other patterns.

Studies have shown that these styles of dealing with caregivers—those most important giants who kept us safe and fed during childhood—tend to carry on in adulthood, and the basic templates adopted then are used to deal with anyone close—partners or friends. Knowing what templates we use, and the templates others use with us, can give us an intellectual understanding of communications issues that allows us to empathize with partners who are driving us crazy with their neediness, or hurting us with their coldness—it's all in the signal-response dynamics of our attachment style. In this book a person will be categorized by their predominant attachment style by referring to their *attachment type*.

Chapter 5

What Type Are You?

First we'll look at your attachment type—which will suggest what type of partner would be good for you, and whether you yourself have some attachment issues you can address to be a better partner to others.

Please go online to take the accurate and self-scoring test by researcher S. Chris Fraley[8] at: http://www.web-research-design.net/ cgi-bin/crq/crq.pl. While you are taking the test, answer the questions with your current partner in mind (if you have one). Then take the test again thinking of yourself before you got together with your current partner; if the two results differ significantly, then your current partner is either making you more or less secure than you would normally be.

The relationship you are thinking of can strongly influence the attachment type you appear to be. "The idea is that when we're with a noncommittal person who's always threatening to leave, we're prone to feel like a clingy, ambivalent child—regardless of our previous attachment experience. When we're with an insecure, punishing nag, we're prone to become somewhat distant and avoidant."[9]

So, while one tends to have a predominant attachment style from childhood experiences, how you behave in a real relationship may vary as the style of your partner influences you. All of us have secure and insecure moments and can temporarily or under stress exhibit any of the patterns.

It is common for those with Avoidant (that is, intermittently-responsive) partners to be driven toward the insecure Anxious-Preoccupied style, while those with Anxious-Preoccupied (over-signalling, clingy) partners are driven to feel more Avoidant themselves.

If you're reading this book, you are likely to be either Secure or Anxious-Preoccupied yourself, with a partner who is either Dismissive-Avoidant or Fearful-Avoidant. If you haven't already read my first book, *Bad Boyfriends,* read the sections which follow to understand the various attachment types, especially the Avoidants (who are especially difficult in intimate relationships.)

Chapter 6

Type: Secure

A person of the secure attachment type (who we will call a *Secure*) is self-confident, empathetic, and observant of the feelings of others. Having been brought up with responsive caregivers and feeling safe in relying on others for comfort and care, the secure person has confidence that she can be herself and disclose her own inner thoughts and feelings to those close to her without fear of rejection—and when she is rejected by someone unfamiliar, know that she is worthwhile and not feel much hurt by others' moods and negative feelings. Confident of her worth, she can roam the emotional world freely and assist others with her strength and empathy; lacking the fears and preoccupations of the other types, she can communicate honestly, empathize completely, and love unconditionally.

How did these people reach their secure state? Some children seem to be naturally resilient, and will find enough good caregivers even in a less-than-ideal childhood to overcome, say, a negligent mother. Others not born with a secure predisposition may achieve it by the attention of responsive but not overbearing parents. And yet others grow into a secure style in adulthood by overcoming their initial, less functional attachment type through therapy, introspection and study, or (most commonly) a significant centering relationship with a partner or a community of friends.

It is the ability to "see" into the feelings of others that separates the secure type most from the others. A quiet, calm attachment center allows the secure person to attune themselves to others, making them better parents, partners, friends, and employees. And the ability to freely express both positive and negative feelings enhances their relationships. This is the skill called *emotional intelligence.*[10]

> If the secure adults had unhappy attachment histories, they seem to have understood and worked them through, at least to the extent that they could speak about them without getting into a stew, often demonstrating insight into the effects their negative experiences had had on them as well as some forgiveness or understanding of the parent's behavior.[11]

> Both Fonagy and Main believe that the most important quality distinguishing the secure from the anxious adults is their capacity to understand what makes themselves and others tick. They are better able to recognize their own inner conflicts and to have a sense of why their parents behaved as they did.[12]

The benefits of the secure style accumulate over a lifetime. Secure children are more liked and have more friends than others, and tend to have happier family lives.

> Kobak found that secure teens—those who were able to speak coherently and thoughtfully about their experiences with their parents—were better able to handle conflicts with both mother and father. They were more assertive and more capable of listening to their parents' point of view. And they showed less dysfunctional, critical anger. They also made an easier transition to college.[13]

Secures find partners and friends more easily, form attachment bonds more readily, and tend to have longer and happier marriages.

In working with others, Secures use their ability to reflect on their own (and others') inner emotional states to more effectively communicate. Their emotional intelligence lets them work in teams, understand the emotional messages sent by others and respond appropriately, both verbally and nonverbally—others understand their feelings better and have a greater sense they can be relied on. Thus, on the whole, Secures are more successful in a group work environment. Secures also have higher incomes, on average.

If you are dating a Secure, he puts his cards on the table, and will show interest if interested, or decline to go forward if not. Secure people don't withhold or manipulate to get what they want—they tell you what they want, and offer what they have to give freely once a relationship is underway. A Secure wants you integrated into his life —he wants his friends and family to be your friends and family, if possible. A Secure does not try to keep you from knowing them, or live a compartmentalized life where you are not welcome in some settings, like work or family. When there is conflict in goals or plans, the Secure will make an effort to understand your point of view and find a compromise that satisfies you both. A Secure does not put up barriers or constantly talk of "boundaries"—if you press on him too hard, the Secure will let you know your error, but not hold it against you. A Secure can speak freely about his feelings and memories, and explain how he feels or felt so you can understand it, and he values your understanding of who he is and how he got to be that way. Secure people tend to show anger in a relationship more easily, but quickly recover their calm and don't hold grudges—someone who is honestly angry at you for a good reason is communicating their distress in a healthy way, when a less secure type might suppress it and add to a secret store of resentments you will never be told about directly.

Levine and Heller have a nice list of the ideal characteristics of Secures:

- Great conflict busters—During a fight they don't feel the need to act defensively or to injure or punish their partner, and so prevent the situation from escalating.
- Mentally flexible—They are not threatened by criticism.

They're willing to reconsider their ways, and if necessary, revise their beliefs and strategies.

- Effective communicators—They expect others to be understanding and responsive, so expressing their feelings freely and accurately to their partners comes naturally to them.
- Not game players—They want closeness and believe others want the same, so why play games?
- Comfortable with closeness, unconcerned about boundaries —They seek intimacy and aren't afraid of being "enmeshed." Because they aren't overwhelmed by a fear of being slighted (as are the anxious) or the need to deactivate (as are the avoidants), they find it easy to enjoy closeness, whether physical or emotional.
- Quick to forgive—They assume their partners' intentions are good and are therefore likely to forgive them when they do something hurtful.
- Inclined to view sex and emotional intimacy as one—They don't need to create distance by separating the two (by being close either emotionally or sexually but not both).
- Treat their partners like royalty—When you've become part of their inner circle, they treat you with love and respect.
- Secure in their power to improve the relationship—They are confident in their positive beliefs about themselves and others, which makes this assumption logical.
- Responsible for their partners' well-being—They expect others to be responsive and loving toward them and so are responsive to others' needs.[14]

Roughly half of the population is secure, but since Secures are more successful at getting into and maintaining happy relationships, Secures are less and less available in older dating pools.

Chapter 7

Type: Anxious-Preoccupied

People of the anxious-preoccupied type (who we will call the *Preoccupied*) are the third-largest attachment type group, at about 20% of the population. Because their early attachment needs were unsatisfied or inconsistently satisfied, they crave intimacy but tend to feel doubtful about their own worth, making it harder for them to trust that they are loved and cared for. At the extremes, and with a more secure or dismissive partner, they are viewed as "needy" or "clingy," and can drive others away by their demands for attention. Many have never been able to come to terms with memories of parental failures:

> Often they spoke as if the feelings of hurt and anger they had as children were as alive in them today as they had been twenty or thirty years before. The childhoods they described were often characterized by intense efforts to please their parents, considerable anger and disappointment, and by role reversals in which the child had tried to parent the adult. But these memories were expressed in a confused and incoherent manner, as if they had never been able to get a grip on what happened to them and integrate it into a comprehensible picture. They seemed still so enmeshed with their parents that infantile feelings flooded and bewildered them as they recalled the past.[15]

Unable to bring their adult understandings to the disappointments of their childhood, they may have created a falsely glowing story to bury the pain of feeling unappreciated:

Anxious adults either failed to have insights into themselves and their parents or offered explanations that were platitudinous, self-deceptive, or self-serving. Thus one anxious [woman], when asked about the relationship between her parents, responded: "I am the apple of my father's eye and... he does absolutely idolize me... and I think it's amazing that my mother has never been remotely jealous of me in any way at all!"[16]

This insecurity is often the result of an insecure parental figure who is herself too needy to allow her child independence with assurance:

A mother who has never worked through her own ambivalent attachment has probably been struggling all her life to find stable love. When she was a child, she may have been pained by the competent, steady caring that she saw friends' parents give to them. As an adult she may be prone to a nagging, uncontrollable jealousy in any close relationships, where she feels cause for doubt. She may want to love deeply and steadily, but it is hard for her because she's never been filled up enough with patient, reliable love to be in a position to give it.... Some preoccupied mothers frequently intrude when the baby is happily exploring on his own and push for interaction even when the baby resists it.... For if a mother unconsciously wishes to keep a baby addicted to her, there is no better strategy than being inconsistently available. Nothing makes a laboratory rat push a pedal more furiously than an inconsistent reward.[17]

The immature, dependent, babyish behavior that Sroufe observed in some ambivalent children may, thus, represent the sort of child his [preoccupied] parent unconsciously wishes for, who will not grow up and separate from mom, who will always be clingy demonstrating his need for her, and who will anxiously seek to appease her. The child, meanwhile, suspended perpetually in his attachment anxieties may, if he gets stuck in his mother's orbit, grow into a similar sort of person, who constantly seeks succor and devotion from another—much more than the average person is likely to put up with.[18]

As preoccupied children grow up, others notice they are too self-centered to quietly listen to emotional messages sent by others, and likely to be unreliable partners in games or work, as in this assessment by fellow students:

> The preoccupied students—embroiled, angry, and incoherent when speaking about their parents—"were seen by their peers as more anxious, introspective, ruminative."[19]

Since they require constant messages of reassurance, the preoccupied find it hard to venture away from their partners or loved ones to accomplish goals, and will undermine their partners if necessary to keep their attention for themselves. The classic clingy child or parent or partner is acting out their anxiety about abandonment:

> [The preoccupied] are hypervigilant about separations, likely to become anxious or even panicky when left, and to be overcome by feelings of clinginess and impotent rage. They do not readily venture forth or take chances, for they do not believe their attachment needs will ever be met. They cling tenaciously to what they have, often using guilt and blame to keep their attachment figures on a short leash.[20]

> Anxious [preoccupied] children learn to manipulate to get their needs met, and invariably their manipulations get carried over into adulthood. The child may become seductive or cute, act fretful, or make others feel guilty for not giving him the attention he wants, all depending on the what strategic styles are modeled or succeed in the family.[21]

In Hazan and Shaver's study, preoccupied adults in a work setting "tended to procrastinate, had difficulty concentrating, and were most distracted by interpersonal concerns. They also had the lowest average income."[22] This inability to concentrate on anything but relationships handicaps the preoccupied, and makes them trouble for teams where they will put their need for reassurance ahead of the task at hand. As a team member, the preoccupied require more management time and attention, and produce less work.

In dating, the preoccupied put their best foot forward and try too hard, sometimes missing the subtle cues that would allow them to listen better to understand their partner's feelings. They feel they must always prove themselves and act to keep your interest—they want constant interaction, constant touch and reassurance, which other types can find maddening. As long as they are getting the attention they want, they will let their partner get away with being difficult in other ways—even negative attention is keeping the touch game going. If their relationships last, it is often because they have found a partner whose insecurities dovetail with theirs, who will participate in a dysfunctional game similar to what they were raised with. While the preoccupied have strong feelings and can discuss them when calm, their feelings are centered around their needs for attention and the failures of others to provide it on demand. They commonly blame others for not understanding their feelings and needs while not feeling safe enough in the relationship to describe them openly. They want to merge with their partner, so this type is prone to codependence—a dysfunctional mutual dependence where neither partner matures further. They are profoundly disturbed by and resist even short separations. The single Preoccupied badly wants a partner and spends a lot of time feeling lonely.

The key to happier relationships for the anxious-preoccupied is working toward an inner feeling of security and independence. This is easier when a Secure partner is present—the reliability of the partner's signalling and response reassures, letting inner security grow. But even the single Preoccupied can take a clue from their type label—they are **preoccupied** with the idea of a relationship. Getting involved with absorbing activities and friendships with others can take their mind off the problem of partner relationships. And self-coaching can help—replacing inner dialog about failings and worries about what others think of you with reassuring self-talk can help prevent overly-clingy and paranoid behavior that drives away significant others. Build confidence in yourself and your value by accomplishing real tasks, and try harder to see things from others' point of view before acting on fears and anger about how they treat you. Soothe your own worries before they trouble others, and have more faith in their goodwill before you assume the worst.

One of the topics Levine and Heller discuss in detail is *hypervigilance* —the anxious-preoccupied are intensely focused on keeping track of the emotional state of desired partners:

> [A study found that people] with an anxious attachment style are indeed more vigilant to changes in others' emotional expression and can have a higher degree of accuracy and sensitivity to other people's cues. However, this finding comes with a caveat. The study showed that people with an anxious attachment style tend to jump to conclusions very quickly, and when they do, they tend to misinterpret people's emotional state. Only when the experiment was designed in such a way that anxious participants had to wait a little longer—they couldn't react immediately when they spotted a change, but had to wait a little longer—and get more information before making a judgment did they have an advantage over other participants.[23]

Hair-trigger misjudgments and mistakes are more likely with this group and can get them into trouble. The anxious-preoccupied should work toward taking the time to consider all the evidence before reacting negatively, so their fine sensitivity to others' emotional states will serve them better.

The anxious-preoccupied will sometimes explain that they feel very strongly and so can't help themselves when overreacting to perceived threats to their relationships. The real explanation for their paranoia is not so much the intensity of feeling, however, as it is their insecurity and lack of understanding and trust in others' good intentions. Because they are so wrapped up in the fear of losing attention or affection, they don't take the time to see matters from the point of view of their significant other and so blunder into misunderstandings and attempts to control their partner through protest behavior.

Levine and Heller describe this behavior well:

> Once activated, they are often consumed with thoughts that have a single purpose: to reestablish closeness with their partner. These thoughts are called activating strategies. Activating strategies are any thoughts or feelings that compel you to get close, physically or emotionally, to your partner. Once he or she responds to you in a way that reestablishes security, you can revert back to your calm, normal self. Activating Strategies:

- Thinking about your mate, difficulty concentrating on other things.
- Remembering only their good qualities.
- Putting them on a pedestal: underestimating your talents and abilities and overestimating theirs.
- An anxious feeling that goes away only when you are in contact with them.
- Believing this is your only chance for love, as in: "I'm only compatible with very few people—what are the chances I'll find another person like him/ her?," or "It takes years to meet someone new; I'll end up alone."

- Believing that even though you're unhappy, you'd better not let go, as in: "If she leaves me, she'll turn into a great partner —for someone else, or "He can change," or "All couples have problems—we're not special in that regard."[24]

Protest behavior is a term originally coined to describe children's screams and cries when separated from their caregiver, now applied by analogy to adult attempts to display unhappiness with a lack of attention or responsiveness from partners. Some protest behavior is part of every relationship—"Hey! You said you'd text me when you got home." But the most clingy, insecure anxious-preoccupied protest so frequently they run the risk of turning off and driving away their partners. When someone is said to be "high maintenance," that means they are excessively needy and need more communication and reassurance than is reasonable.

Levine and Heller have a good list of Protest Behaviors:

- Calling, texting, or e-mailing many times, waiting for a phone call, loitering by your partner's workplace in hopes of running into him/ her.
- Withdrawing: Sitting silently "engrossed" in the paper, literally turning your back on your partner, not speaking, talking with other people on the phone and ignoring him/ her.
- Keeping score: Paying attention to how long it took them to return your phone call and waiting just as long to return theirs; waiting for them to make the first "make-up" move and acting distant until such time.
- Acting hostile: Rolling your eyes when they speak, looking away, getting up and leaving the room while they're talking (acting hostile can transgress to outright violence at times).
- Threatening to leave: Making threats—" We're not getting along, I don't think I can do this anymore," "I knew we weren't really right for each other," "I'll be better off without

you"—all the while hoping [partner] will stop you from leaving.

- Manipulations: Acting busy or unapproachable. Ignoring phone calls, saying you have plans when you don't.
- Making him/her feel jealous: Making plans to get together with an ex for lunch, going out with friends to a singles bar, telling your partner about someone who hit on you today.[25]

Protest behaviors are intended to force a reassuring response from the partner—and resorting to them too frequently is bad for any relationship.

Chapter 8

Type: Fearful-Avoidant

The fearful-avoidant (sometimes called anxious-avoidant) share an underlying distrust of caregiving others with the dismissive-avoidant, but have not developed the armor of high self-esteem to allow them to do without attachment; they realize the need for and want intimacy, but when they are in a relationship that starts to get close, their fear and mistrust surfaces and they distance. In psychology this is called an approach-avoidance conflict[26]; at a distance the sufferer wants to get closer, but when he does, the fear kicks in and he wants to withdraw. This leads to a pattern of circling or cycling, and the fearful-avoidant can often be found in a series of short relationships ended by their finding fault with a partner who seems more threatening as the partner gets closer to understanding.

The early caregiving of a fearful-avoidant type often has some features of both neglect and abuse (which may be psychological—a demeaning or absent caregiver, rejection and teasing from early playmates.) A fearful-avoidant type both desires close relationships and finds it difficult to be truly open to intimacy with others out of fear of rejection and loss, since that is what he or she has received from caregivers. Instead of the dismissive's defense mechanism of going it alone and covering up feelings of need for others by developing high self-esteem, the fearful-avoidant subconsciously believe there is something unacceptable about them that makes anyone who knows them deeply likely to reject or betray them, so they will find reasons to relieve this fear by distancing anyone who gets too close. As with the dismissive, the fearful-avoidant will have difficulty understanding the emotional lives of others, and empathy, while present, is not very strong—thus there will be poor communication of feelings with his partner.

> Both Ainsworth and Main found the mother of the avoidant child to be distant—rejecting of the infant's attachment needs, hostile to signs of dependency, and disliking affectionate, face-to-face physical contact, especially when the baby desired it. Her aversion to nurturance would seem to be a logical outgrowth of the neglect she probably experienced when she herself was young. Needs and longings that were painfully unmet have become a source of hurt and shame for her. Having cut herself off from them, they make her angry, depressed, or disgusted when she sees them in her child.[27]

A narcissistic or demanding mother can cause a child to mold him- or herself to please the parent to the point where little remains of the child's own feelings and personality; they have been trained to display a false personality to gain parental approval.

Children who have been brought up this way often become high-achieving, competent adults with a sense of hollowness at the core, and episodic low self-esteem. They are often from families where parents are highly competent and have high expectations, and parenting may have been so active that childhood selves were quashed by parental expectations, judgments, and signals. In other words, parental ego is so dominant that the child's true feelings are buried to avoid their disapproval. What the child learns to display is a false persona more pleasing to the active and admired parents. Some authors, notably Alice Miller, have called such parenting "abuse," though it is abuse through disapproval and verbal rejection of behavior the caregiver disliked.[28]

While we all have public faces—versions of ourselves edited for public consumption—the fearful-avoidant have commonly developed a *false self,* an acceptable outer personality which inhibits spontaneous display of their innermost thoughts and feelings even in intimacy. Those who think of themselves as their friends will often be surprised and hurt when high stress brings out the true personality of the masked one. By hiding their true selves, such people live with a social support network that has been attracted by their fake persona, so that when a crisis occurs, those who might have cared for them aren't around, and those who are around don't care for the real person revealed by the crisis. In a quotation commonly misattributed to Dr. Seuss (but actually a modified quote from Bernard Baruch), "Be who you are and say what you feel, because those who mind don't matter and those who matter don't mind." Real intimacy and loyalty are founded on honesty, and pretending to be someone you aren't—keeping up appearances—leaves you with no lasting close friends or partners.

A fairy tale that is a parable for the warped attachment views of the avoidant:

> There was once a dreadfully wicked hobgoblin. One day he had a simply marvelous idea. He was going to make a looking glass that would reflect everything that was good and beautiful in such a way that it would look dreadful or at least not very important. When you looked in it, you would not be able to see any of the good or the beautiful in yourself or in the world. Instead, this looking glass would reflect everything that was bad or ugly and make it look very important. The most beautiful landscapes would look like heaps of garbage, and the best people would look repulsive or would seem stupid. People's faces would be so changed that they could not be recognized, and if there was anything that a person was ashamed of or wanted to hide, you could be sure that this would be just the thing that the looking glass emphasized.

> The hobgoblin set about making this looking glass, and when he was finished, he was delighted with what he had done.

Anyone who looked into it could only see the bad and the ugly, and all that was good and beautiful in the world was distorted beyond recognition.

One day the hobgoblin's assistants decided to carry the looking glass up to the heavens so that even the angels would look into it and see themselves as ugly and stupid. They hoped that perhaps even God himself would look into it! But, as they reached the heavens, a great invisible force stopped them and they dropped the dreadful looking glass. And as it fell, it broke into millions of pieces.

And now came the greatest misfortune of all. Each of the pieces was hardly as large as a grain of sand, and they flew about all over the world. If anyone got a bit of glass in his eye there it stayed, and then he would see everything as ugly or distressing. Everything good would look stupid. For every tiny splinter of the glass possessed the same power that the whole glass had!

Some people got a splinter in their hearts, and that was dreadful, too, for then their hearts turned into lumps of ice and could no longer feel love.

The hobgoblin watched all this and he laughed until his sides ached. And still the tiny bits of glass flew about, And now we will hear all about it....

—from The Snow Queen, Hans Christian Andersen

Chapter 9

Type: Dismissive-Avoidant

Much of what follows also applies to the fearful-avoidant, who can be thought of as the avoidant who haven't given up. The term "avoidant" is used to discuss characteristics shared by both the dismissive-avoidant and the fearful-avoidant.

The two avoidant types (dismissive-avoidant and fearful-avoidant) share a subconscious fear that caregivers are not reliable and intimacy is a dangerous thing. The dismissive-avoidant individuals (who we will call *Dismissives*) have completed a mental transformation that says: "I am good, I don't need others, and they aren't really important to me. I am fine as I am," while the fearful-avoidant are still consciously craving an intimacy which scares them when it actually happens. Both types were trained not to rely on caregivers, but the Dismissive has dealt with this by deciding he doesn't need others much at all, and so has little apparent reason to participate in the emotional signaling of a close relationship.

Dismissives are rarely open about declaring themselves contemptuous of others. But they think highly of themselves and will tell you they value their self-sufficiency and independence—needing others is weak, feelings of attachment are strings that hold you down, empathy and sympathy are for lesser creatures.

A Dismissive often has a story of a previous relationship which was never fully realized or ended when his partner left—early in his romantic life, or perhaps long-distance. The memory of this idealized previous partner is used as a weapon when the Dismissive tires—as they quickly do—of a real relationship and its demands; no one could measure up to the one that got away. This is another distancing trick to keep real intimacy at bay.

Dismissives have poor access to early emotional memories, having built a defensive shield of self-esteem and self-sufficiency that requires negative memories to be suppressed:

> Adults characterized as "dismissing of attachment" seemed unable or unwilling to take attachment issues seriously. They answered questions in a guarded way, without much elaboration, and often had trouble remembering their childhoods. They seemed to dislike and distrust looking inward. Some exhibited an underlying animosity that seemed to imply: "Why are you asking me to dredge up this stuff?" or "The whole point of this interview is stupid!" The dismissing adults spoke vaguely about their parents, frequently describing them in idealized terms. But when pressed for incidents that might illustrate such descriptions, their memories contradicted their assessments, as negative facts leaked into their narratives. Thus, one [dismissive] called his mother "nice" but eventually revealed that she was often drunk and swore at him. When asked if that bothered him, he replied, "Not at all. That's what made me the strong person I am today. I'm not like those people at work who have to hold [each other's] hands before making a decision."

This stalwart, anti-sniveling response was typical of the way dismissing subjects played down the affect of early hurts or embraced them as having built their character. Another [dismissive] described his mother as "loving," "caring," "the world's most affectionate person," "invariably available to her children," "an institution." But pressed for details, he could not recall a single instance of his mother's warmth or nurturance.[29]

Fellow students recognized the hostility and mistrust of the dismissive:

> The dismissing freshmen—who had trouble remembering early experiences with their parents and played down the importance of attachments issues in their interviews—"were seen by their peers as more hostile, more condescending, more distant."[30]

The buried need for emotional attachment is not consciously felt by dismissives, but their need for others can show itself unconsciously:

> If a spouse is away for a period of time, it is natural to miss him. If a move is made to a new place, it is natural to feel a loss over friends and family who have been left behind and to work assiduously to create new ties to replace the old. But with separations, too, anxious attachment can deform the process. Clinical work suggests that people with what appears to be an avoidant or dismissive psychology often fail to recognize that separations have an emotional impact in them. ... When a spouse is away, a person with this psychology may become obsessively focused on work, may even celebrate the separation as an opportunity to get more work done, but then be strangely, perhaps even cruelly distant from the spouse when he or she returns.[31]

Dismissives will learn to get their needs for attention, sex, and community met through less demanding partners who fail to require real reciprocation or intimacy (often the anxious-preoccupied!):

> An avoidantly attached boy [...] will probably learn to disguise his care seeking, He may become adept at using various forms of control to get another person to be there for him; he may seek out people whose needs are more apparent and who give without having to be asked.[32]

Avoidants "were most likely to be workaholics and most inclined to allow work to interfere with social life. Some said they worked too hard to have time for socializing, others that they preferred to work alone. Not surprisingly, their incomes were as high as the secures, but their satisfaction was as low as [the preoccupied.]"[33] Because of their ability to focus on work and act independently, dismissives can be phenomenal explorers and individual contributors. In fields where performance is not based on group efforts, and a lack of concern for others' feelings can actually be beneficial, the dismissive can be a star player—for example, in some types of litigation, or some scientific fields.

In dating, avoidants can be charming and have learned all the social graces—they often know how they are expected to act in courtship and can play the role well for a time. But lacking a positive view of attached others, they expect relationships to fulfill a romantic ideal which no real human being can create for them, so all fall short and are discarded when it becomes inconvenient to continue. Typically as the relationship ages, avoidants will begin to find fault and focus on petty shortcomings of their partner. Because they are not really aware of their own feelings, they can't talk about them in a meaningful way, and often the first clue the about-to-be-dumped have that something is wrong is the avoidant's move to break up with them. Once you have read this book, you will likely be aware of the missing signals and the many small clues that the avoidant is not committing to you or anyone any time soon, but those who are unaware of this type will usually soldier on, not trusting their own feeling that something about Prince Charming is not quite right.

The dismissive-avoidant is afraid of and incapable of tolerating true intimacy. Since he was brought up not to depend on anyone or reveal feelings that might not be acceptable to caregivers, his first instinct when someone gets really close to him is to run away. Superficially the dismissive (as opposed to the fearful-avoidant) thinks very highly of himself, and is likely to pin any blame for relationship troubles on his partners; but underneath (especially in the extreme form we label narcissism), there is such low self esteem that at his core he does not feel his true self is worthy of love and attention. Should a partner penetrate his armor, unconscious alarm bells go off and he retreats to either aloneness or the safety of companionship with others who do not realize he is not what he appears to be on the surface.

The avoidant types are the least likely to form a positive attachment bond with their partners, and the Dismissive flavor especially tend to be single or rapidly go through partners, since their psyche refuses to recognize any dependency on the bond and suppresses any feelings of love and attachment. Both types are almost never found coupled with another avoidant person, since in such a relationship there is no one to start the signaling cycle that keeps a relationship going. At least Fearful-Avoidant types are aware that they need attachment and are more likely to be reachable by a secure or preoccupied person, but with the unfortunate tendency to end relationships because they subconsciously fear rejection and would rather reject first; and they also have the general avoidant tendency to not feel love or other attachment emotions very consciously.

The Dismissive attempts to limit his level of exposure to partners by manipulating his response, commonly by failing to respond to messages requesting assurance. Dismissives let you know that you are low on their priority list, and your inner emotional state is your problem—when you are with one, you are really still alone, in an attachment sense. By only partly participating in the normal message-response of the attached, they subconsciously limit the threat another poses to their independence. This behavior is called *distancing*, and all of us do it to limit our intimacy with others when we don't want to be as close as they do, but for the dismissive it's a tool to be used on the most important people in their lives.

Levine and Heller have a useful list of distancing behaviors (also called deactivating strategies):

- Saying (or thinking) "I'm not ready to commit"—but staying together nonetheless, sometimes for years.
- Focusing on small imperfections in your partner: the way s/he talks, dresses, eats, or (fill in the blank) and allowing it to get in the way of your romantic feelings.
- Pining after an ex-girlfriend or boyfriend—(the "phantom ex"...).
- Flirting with others—a hurtful way to introduce insecurity into the relationship.
- Not saying "I love you"—while implying that you do have feelings toward the other person.
- Pulling away when things are going well (e.g., not calling for several days after an intimate date).
- Forming relationships with an impossible future, such as with someone who is married.
- "Checking out mentally" when your partner is talking to you.
- Keeping secrets and leaving things foggy—to maintain your feeling of independence.
- Avoiding physical closeness—e.g., not wanting to share the same bed, not wanting to have sex, walking several strides ahead of your partner.[34]

The more extreme avoidants are almost incapable of talking about their feelings; whatever feelings they do have access to are primarily negative and they have great difficulty describing them verbally.

This syndrome is called *alexithymia*[35], the roots of the word literally meaning "having no words for feelings," which is not at all the same thing as not having feelings. The worst cases can only express themselves with inchoate rages and tantrums, or unexplained physical symptoms like stomach pains and adrenalin rushes.

The most compelling theory of how consciousness arose has

between-person communication (primitive language) giving rise to internal communication, so that what we see as a stream of consciousness is actually internal dialogue, talking to yourself. Noting this, you might say that an inability to name and talk about feelings cripples a person's ability to be consciously aware of them. If one is very poor at doing this, one would tend to note feelings only as manifested in somatic symptoms like fast heart rate, discomfort, loss of energy, nervousness, etc.

This is why talking to someone about how you feel (or writing about it) is also training for being conscious of feelings internally. The more you talk about it to others, the more you can talk about it to yourself. Even for those not suffering from alexithymia, talking or writing about feelings can clarify understanding of them, which is one of the reasons talk therapy is effective.

Chapter 10

Type Combinations in Couples

Secure with Secure:

These couples may well have other problems (addiction, differences over money and spending, fairy-tale expectations [see "The Destructive Fairy Tale Model," later]), but on the whole since they are both Secure, they tend to communicate well and don't end up in the dysfunctional communication patterns as often. Having their own internal sense of security makes them less self-centered, and allows greater empathy for their partner's feelings. A sense of reasonableness and fairness makes every issue they face a bit easier to face together, and counting on each other is more often rewarded.

Anxious-Preoccupied with Secure:

The Preoccupied will test the patience of the Secure by requiring more messages of reassurance and edging toward anxiety when the Secure can't respond quickly or reassuringly. This will tend to drive the Secure toward a more dismissive attachment *style* in interactions —despite possessing internal security, the excessive demands of the Preoccupied would make anyone less patient. If this problem is not too severe, the secure partner can bring the preoccupied partner further toward security by constant patient reassurance, even when the Preoccupied one is being unreasonably demanding.

The secure partner will sometimes feel alone in carrying most of the responsibility for the relationship's emotional stability. In crisis, the

Preoccupied will revert to anxiety and self-centeredness, and that will feel to the Secure like partner flakeout. If the relationship does well and the preoccupied partner grows more secure in time, this problem will ease.

Dismissive-Avoidant with Secure:

The Dismissive will tend to drive the secure partner toward attachment anxiety by failing to respond well or at all to reasonable messages requesting reassurance. As with the Preoccupied, an extremely secure partner can gradually move the insecure partner toward more security, but at great cost in patience and effort. If the Dismissive recognizes the problem and takes some responsibility for trying to respond positively even when he doesn't really feel like it, this can gradually reorient the dismissive partner toward more satisfying couples communication. If this does not happen, a Secure is more likely to give up on the relationship and move on, since unlike the Preoccupied who often stick with bad relationships, the Secure partner knows someone better is out there and is not too afraid to give up on a losing relationship.

Fearful-Avoidant with Secure:

This has some similarities with the Dismissive-Secure pairing, but the lower self-esteem of the Fearful-Avoidant makes it more likely he or she will be the one to exit the relationship when it becomes intimate and routine, since the closer they get to a real person the more afraid they are of loss, and apparently rationalizing their exit as due to their partner's flaws is less painful than they subconsciously imagine being rejected by their partner would be.

Dismissive-Avoidant with Anxious-Preoccupied:

This is a classic long-lasting but dysfunctional pairing. The two types (one under-valuing attachment and one over-valuing attachment) create an interlocking dependency full of stress and anxiety for both. Because the Dismissive may actually prefer having his/her view of others as needy and clingy confirmed, and comforted by controlling the relationship by doling out just enough responsiveness to keep the preoccupied partner off-balance but on the hook, the Dismissive may settle in for the long haul, while the preoccupied partner is unhappy with settling for crumbs but sticks around out of fear of being alone, afraid of never finding another relationship.

This is one of the most common (second only to Secure-Secure) long-lasting relationship types. More on this couple type coming up in the chapter "Anxious-Preoccupied with Avoidant."

Fearful-Avoidant with Anxious-Preoccupied:

Somewhat like the Dismissive-Preoccupied pairing, but less stable; the avoidant partner will be less comfortable with the constant requests for reassurance from the Preoccupied partner and will be less likely to tolerate a long relationship spent fending off intimacy. If the avoidant partner allows real closeness to develop, that triggers his or her anxiety; if they stay at a distance, the preoccupied partner will be unhappy and increase the level of requests.

Anxious-Preoccupied with Anxious-Preoccupied:

A match that usually ends badly and quickly as neither partner is good at anticipating the needs of the other since they are preoccupied with their own attachment needs.. It's not impossible that two mildly preoccupied individuals will bond and learn to satisfy each other's security needs, but it is rare.

Fearful-Avoidant with Dismissive-Avoidant:

Uncommon, since neither avoidant type is very good at positive attachment. While one might think both types would prefer to be with more distancing partners, the Fearful-Avoidant is not comfortable without some intimacy and would find the Dismissive's lack of positive messaging as anxiety-inducing as the other types. Meanwhile, the Dismissive partner doesn't get as much ego-boosting attention as he or she would from another type, and so this combination is less likely to even get started.

Dismissive-Avoidant with Dismissive-Avoidant:

...and even more so for this very rare combination. Without a partner willing to do some of the communications work, this couple type rarely even gets started, and the "why bother?" from both of them tends to end it quickly under even minor stresses.

Chapter 11

A Note on Codependence

Codependence is an overused term implying that normal partner interdependence is somehow dysfunctional.

The concept and terminology came out of the Alcoholics Anonymous movement; the addicted were seen as trapped in a web of dependency with others (their *enablers,* or codependents) who made excuses for and assisted the addicts in avoiding the consequences of their addiction, making their impaired life seem more normal and postponing the ultimate reckoning that would force the addicts to change their lives.

Pop psychologists and media spread this idea far and wide, and today almost any relationship can be tagged "codependent," as if the unitary self-sufficiency of the dismissive was the ideal state and any reliance on others weak and unhealthy. Of course a close relationship has features of mutual dependency! So when do we begin to call interdependence dysfunctional? One key may be purpose: is the interdependence advancing the capabilities of both of the partners, or is it creating a stagnant holding pattern that is preventing further growth? The highest interdependence of all occurs between parents and child; but this is a temporary state where effective parenting is creating an independent adult who will ideally function well in the world. Spouses and close friends may pine for each other when apart, yet their mutual emotional support allows them to achieve and further their own development.

It certainly happens that feelings of attachment between, for example, a narcissist and his current enabler create a dysfunctional holding pattern keeping reality from harming the narcissist's fragile self-regard. This also happens when an alcoholic is shielded by her husband from the consequences of her addiction until it is too late. Hoping against all reasonable hope that the pattern will change and trying to pretend that you can keep harm from your loved one by covering up problems and placing their short-term feelings above what would actually be best for them, and yourself, is a mistake we can all understand and sympathize with. That is what dysfunctional codependence looks like.

Avoidants, particularly the dismissive-avoidant, flee to their Fortress of Solitude when intimacy turns threatening, and it is with them that the fad for declaring relationships codependent causes the most trouble. It is not unusual for a Dismissive to explain to his current romantic partner that he finds her desire for responses and attention to be "codependent." It's an all-purpose rationalization suggesting that partners owe each other only what limited attention and care they can spare from their busy lifestyles.

The "just when needed, just the right amount" principle of responsiveness is ideal between the best partners, and best friends. For the avoidant types, a willingness to tolerate some dependence on significant others is a sign of improvement; and for the severely anxious-preoccupied, being able to leave their partner be when he's busy without starting to worry is a sign of growing security.

Part Three

Avoidants in Relationships

Chapter 12

What Love Looks Like to Avoidants

Dismissive-Avoidants are the hard cases: convinced that love is a foolish notion designed to entrap the weak in the dependency they hate. But even the Fearful-Avoidant tend to believe less in the possibilities of romantic love for the long term, often because their experience has been that it doesn't last and is inevitably disappointing —having rationalized their way into ending many relationships because their partner wasn't good enough, they start to think they are either very unlucky or there aren't any candidates up to their exacting standards. As a variety of self-fulfilling prophecy, their pessimism is justified. "[A]voidant people were more likely to believe that love either does not exist or is likely to disappear once a relationship is formed.... Avoidant people find it harder to fall in love and many even doubt that such a state is possible outside of movies and romantic stories. Even within a long-term relationship, anxious people are more likely to sustain their 'passion,' whereas an avoidant attachment style is associated with experiencing less passion over time."[36]

Subconsciously, Dismissives do seek out attachment, though consciously they tell themselves that they want sex or a convenient helpmate; their conscious attitude is that some of their practical and immediate needs will be filled by a compliant partner. They can be very charming and persuasive, and for the less experienced or the quick-to-attach Anxious-Preoccupied, filling their needs can seem rewarding for a time. But the lack of real affection and feeling will show itself in unresponsiveness, and if pushed, passive-aggressive contempt, verbal, or even physical abuse. The Dismissive wants to have his needs met, but yours are not very important to him or her. Yet we know they are often somatically affected by separations and loss of loved ones; it's just that these feelings are repressed and denied at a conscious level. Does a Dismissive love their partner? The answer may be "yes, but they don't know it."

The Fearful-Avoidant consciously seek out relationships and know they want to be with someone, but can't control the urge to escape when their partner gets really close to them; it increases their anxiety to be truly *known*. Since they have never experienced a feeling of safety when completely open and intimate with a partner, they tend to see love as a theoretical goal and a need, but their anxiety has kept them from really experiencing it. If they got very close to someone, they subconsciously believe that someone would hurt or abandon them—so they find a way to get away from them first.

> Overall, then, attachment insecurity is associated with less constructive attitudes toward romantic love. Avoidant deactivating strategies seem to inhibit romantic and altruistic forms of love and favor game playing or practicality rather than romance. Consistent with this conclusion, R. W. Doherty, Hatfield, Thompson, and Choo (1994) found that more avoidant people scored lower on scales assessing passionate (erotic) and companionate (agapic) forms of love.[37]

Chapter 13

Avoidants: Emotional Repression

Avoidants are known to be viscerally effected by events that would normally trigger conscious emotions—such events are often reflected in a racing heart, disturbed digestion, and poor sleep even when the avoidant (Dismissive-Avoidant especially) consciously feels nothing —and will tell you he or she doesn't really mind that their partner is gone, for example, since it's such a great opportunity to get more work done away from the partner's demands for attention.

This blockade on attachment-related emotions is a defense mechanism; it was necessary in childhood to survive a caregiver's inattention or abuse. The feelings of being unloved and unwanted that might otherwise have destroyed the child's will to live are shunted aside and never reach a conscious level; avoidants tend to have poor memories of emotional events and report unreliably when asked about their childhoods.

An interesting post on the blog StopTheStorm discusses this phenomenon:

> When it comes to thinking about, describing and feeling emotions, I always have a sideline running in the background concerning my father. I think about the dismissive-avoidant insecure attachment disorder patterns as researchers are now being able to actually see them operate through visually watching the brains of such people.

> Researchers can watch how some brains create in effect a

firewall that leaves actual emotions as they ARE triggered in the body completely out of conscious awareness. Researchers can see the emotion being experienced in the brain AND at the same time be screened from a person so that they do not know they are even there—AT ALL. The brain is consuming massive amounts of energy during this screening process, and these 'brain-holders' never know it.

There are specific early caregiver-to-infant interactions that create these brains from birth to age one. These changed brains are intimately connected to the changed nervous system and body of their 'holders'. Being cared for by unresponsive, unemotional, cold, depressed and 'blank-faced' caregivers are some of the ways these dismissive-avoidant brains are created in infants from the beginning.

These same infants, had they been interacted with by securely attached and appropriate-adequate early caregivers would have developed entirely different brains. My father was an unwanted infant born to an unwilling and depressed mother, raised by his teenage sister primarily who was not caring or nurturing. In the end, my father's dismissive-avoidant insecurely attached brain worked very well on his behalf as he could NOT FEEL— did not HAVE to feel—and hence could ignore what he NEEDED to pay attention to and react to appropriately.

I have an important person I care deeply about who I believe also has a dismissive-avoidant insecure attachment disorder, and I can see how easily this pattern fits with Narcissistic Personality Disorder. Very nicely indeed. The fact is that people who fit into this range can most often manage to get along just fine—but have extremely limited (if any) ability to FEEL and therefore to CARE how others feel, either. It would be easy to call them 'intimacy disabled'.[38]

One of the better studies of brain activation in avoidants concluded:

> As a whole, these brain imaging data support but also extend the notion... that attachment avoidance is associated with a preferential use of emotion suppression in interpersonal/social contexts. Furthermore, they reveal that reappraisal may not work for these individuals, leading to impaired down-regulation of amygdala reactivity. This pattern may help understand why avoidantly attached individuals tend to become highly emotional when their preferred regulation strategies fail or cannot be employed.[39]

Translated, when deactivating strategies (intended to reduce the importance of an attachment relationship to the avoidant) fail to work or can't be used, the avoidant can be overwhelmed by unprocessed feelings that are normally blocked or avoided. The avoidant's strategy is to never be put into a position where deep feelings of loss might break out by distancing anyone who gets too close and minimizing the importance of attached others.

Chapter 14

Avoidants as Caregivers

"Every man for him- (or her-) self"—this is the slogan of the Dismissive. While they may take some pains to hide it, they truly aren't very empathetic or caring, and when someone in need asks for their help, it may be given grudgingly and only to keep the approval of others who observe them. This isn't because they are completely unable to empathize, but because their lifelong habit is to resist being drawn closer to others by mutual need, and helping someone would mean getting closer to them than feels safe. The empathy they do feel is blocked by rationalizations that distance them from those they might assist.

> Avoidant people, who often maintain what they perceive to be a safe distance from their partners, are likely to react coolly or unresponsively to suffering partners and try to avoid being taken advantage of or "sucked in." Avoidant people do not generally approve of expressions of need and vulnerability, whether their own or those of their partners, and they have no desire to get entangled with someone whose weaknesses and needs are all too visible. For them, besides being a potential drain on their own resources, a suffering person threatens to mirror their own suppressed weaknesses and vulnerabilities.[40]

Avoidants need to feel separated from and superior to someone in need; any similarity between another's needs and his own needs is to be denied or the avoidant feels threatened by the recognition of his own vulnerability implied by responding supportively. So when they do help, it is often with a superior attitude:

Studies… show that avoidant people project their own negative qualities onto others, then distance themselves from both the qualities and the people thought to possess them. When obliged by social norms or interpersonal commitments to help others, avoidant people are likely to express disapproval, to lack sympathy and compassion, and to behave insensitively. At times, their reactions to others' suffering may take the form of pity rather than sympathy or compassion. Pity portrays the sufferer as inferior to oneself and causes a person either to withdraw rather than help or to help while showing disgust or disdain (Ben-Zeev, 1999). In some cases, avoidant people's negative models of others and associated hostile attitudes toward them… may even transform pity into gloating (i.e., actually enjoying another person's suffering; "The idiot is being stewed in his own juices"; "He made his bed, now let him lie in it"). This is the motive behind hostile, dismissive humor—avoidant people's most characteristic form of humor (Kazarian & Martin, 2004; Saroglou & Scariot, 2002).[41]

Breaking the extreme avoidant out of this pattern is very difficult. As we'll see later in chapter 35, "Teaching Avoidants to Use Empathy," explaining to a more thoughtful avoidant how their dismissive style harms those they love and requesting they spend time considering the feelings of their loved ones before acting may increase their ability to empathize and respond supportively. It's a habit that pays off in increased happiness for everyone near them and ultimately for them as well.

Chapter 15

Avoidants as Parents

As we have seen, avoidants tend to be unresponsive to partner needs and unconcerned with the negative effect their lack of supportive communication has on their partners. How much does this lack of caring extend to their care for children? If you are married with children, you may have observed moments of caring interaction with them, but not as often as perhaps might be appropriate; and studies have shown that the typical avoidant is a somewhat negligent, emotionally distant parent:

> Edelstein et al. (2004) videotaped children's and parents' behavior when each of the children received an inoculation at an immunization clinic, and found that more avoidant parents (assessed with a self-report scale) were less responsive to their children, particularly if the children became highly distressed; that is, when the children were most upset and most in need of parental support, avoidant parents failed to provide effective care.[42]

The dynamics that make the Dismissive/Anxious-Preoccupied partnership so unsatisfying are repeated with children who try to get more attention from an avoidant parent. A child either learns not to expect emotional support (thus growing more avoidant themselves) or falls into the trap of requesting more and being brutally rebuffed by a parent who sees their needs as weaknesses to be despised:

> As expected, avoidant individuals exhibited a neglectful, nonresponsive style of caregiving. They scored relatively low on

proximity maintenance and sensitivity, reflecting their tendency to maintain distance from a needy partner (restricting accessibility, physical contact, and sensitivity), and tended to adopt a controlling, uncooperative stance resembling their domineering behavior in other kinds of social interactions....[43]

Over time, children with an avoidant parent will look to their other parent for support. If the other parent is a sensitive caregiver, the child will model future attachment styles on that parent; but if the other parent is, for example, anxious-preoccupied, the child will more likely end up with some variety of insecure attachment type. Between the Scylla of the coldhearted dismissive and the Charybdis of the clingy, preoccupied parent, the child will not have a healthy model to work with.

If your partner is avoidant and you have had or intend to have children, it is especially important that you provide a good model of caregiving: there when needed, and only when needed; calm, cheerful, responsive, but not hovering. Consider carefully (if it's not too late) how you might encourage your avoidant spouse to handle your children's needs with more attention and care; and if you are considering bringing up children in the critical years from birth to age 2, whether it might be wise to wait until either your partner has learned to be more supportive or you have found a better partner. Because a steady parent's love and attention is so important to the healthy emotional development of children, if you find you can't be the steady one to give your children a good model because you yourself are off-balance from your avoidant partner's lack of support, do what you have to do to make the environment better. It's not just your current suffering that you should worry about—your children may suffer a lifetime of attachment dysfunction as well.

Here's a report from a mother who has just about had it with both her husband and her dad, who show the same dismissive pattern:

My son was crying last night as he talked about how he could not ever talk to his dad about anything. I very much relate and I have great compassion for him. I want to be stronger for HIM.

This morning I went to the gym and there was some show about weddings. The fathers were walking the daughter down the aisle, so proud. Then the other day I saw an ad about graduation... again, the fathers were so proud standing right next to their daughters.

It hurts very badly. I recall inviting my dad to my college graduation and he said he had to work. He doesn't care that I was with an abusive man in my marriage. Instead he speaks so highly of him, how he is the father of his grandchildren (who he can't stand and had nothing nice to say about)...

Once when we were visiting, my son (then 10) had a febrile seizure. I told my dad I was taking him to the doctor. My dad criticized me for overreacting. When my older son had a seizure at 5 years old from a high fever, my stepmom acted like I overreacted when I took him to the ER.[44]

And this adult survivor of dismissive parenting talks about how it felt:

My father is passive abusive. His emotional abuse is very covert. Mostly he just doesn't care, doesn't listen when I talk to him, doesn't know anything about me, my life or my kids because he doesn't care to know and he doesn't listen to anyone who tries to tell him. To the general public, (and according to my siblings) my father is regarded as this 'nice' guy and he is never violent, never mean and never hurtful with his words, but the truth is that his relationship style is dismissive and disinterested all of which is very hurtful. I spent many years in childhood and in adulthood 'begging' (in all kinds of ways) my emotionally abusive father to notice me. The fact that he didn't was and is very hurtful. There is a very loud message that is delivered to me when I am disregarded. The message is that I don't matter, that I am not important, that I am not worth listening to and that I don't have anything to contribute to his life. My father is emotionally unavailable, and that is very hurtful. Love is an action and love doesn't damage self-esteem. Love doesn't define a 'loved one' as insignificant.

After years of trying to tell my passive abusive father that his constant cutting me off whenever I tried to tell him about me, and that his lack of interest in my life was a problem for me— and due to the fact that there wasn't any change on his part, I gave up; I finally realized that he wasn't going to change."[45]

Chapter 16

Avoidants as Life Partners

So we've seen that avoidants (especially the dismissive-avoidant) think the idea of love is a snare or a delusion; that they view relationships as a way of getting their sexual and practical needs met, not an equal partnership of mutual caring and support; that they are negligent caregivers and bad parents who treat their children as irritants and nonentities. It's not looking too good for them as supportive partners, spouses, or even friends. Having been denied supportive caregiving in their childhood, they have blocked the feelings of nurturance that are required to support others, and the result is a self-centered, insensitive partner:

> There is also evidence that more avoidant people report having less positive feelings toward a romantic partner after outperforming the partner, or being outperformed by him or her, on cognitive tasks (Scinta & Gable, 2005). That is, avoidant people tend to bask in the glow of a superior performance even if this basking damages a romantic partner's self-worth. Moreover, they tend to deny their partners the benefits of a successful performance. Overall, it seems that avoidant individuals' narcissistic tendencies, lack of nurturance, and deficits in interpersonal sensitivity inhibit or distort expressions of positive regard for a romantic partner.…[46]

Even a Secure will have problems maintaining their sense of security in a relationship with an avoidant. If mutual happiness comes from a sense of teamwork and communication to solve both internal and external problems, what is the result when one member of the team refuses to help out emotionally most of the time? Relationships between an avoidant and another person tend to be unsatisfying and unhappy. This means these relationships are more likely to end, and end more quickly (except for the reinforcing dismissive/anxious-preoccupied pairing, which can be quite long-lived.) What do the studies show?:

> Even if attachment insecurity is conducive to relationship dissatisfaction, does it also contribute over time to breakups and divorces? The answer to this question appears to be "yes." In the very first study of romantic attachment, Hazan and Shaver (1987) found that people who described themselves as having an avoidant or anxious attachment style had shorter relationships (4.9 and 6 years, respectively) than secure people (10 years) and were more likely to report having been divorced (10% of anxious and 12% of avoidant participants vs. 6% of secure participants).... In a study of individuals who entered another marriage following a divorce, the avoidant ones were more likely to divorce again (Ceglian & Gardner, 1999).[47]

Avoidants of both types exit relationships more readily and with fewer regrets; they often feel a sense of relief at leaving their "overly demanding" (that is, intimacy-seeking) partner, only to take up with a compliant new one who is very similar to start the cycle again. If their partner puts up with their distancing and satisfies their other needs, they may stay for a long term; but if anything goes wrong they are not the loyal types who will stay, "for richer or poorer, in sickness and in health"—when you hear about a spouse divorcing their partner with cancer, that's often what's going on.

> Kirkpatrick and Hazan's (1994) findings for avoidant individuals suggested, in contrast, they these people were ready to exit a close relationship as soon as they experienced relationship distress. They were the most likely of the three attachment "types" (assessed in that study with a categorical

self-report measure) to report no longer being involved with a partner 4 years later.[48]

Avoidant individuals are especially likely to be dissatisfied with their relationships (when they are in them) and to address their dissatisfaction by leaving.[49]

When their relationships are unhappy, the avoidant rarely resort to violent abuse; they are much more likely to use the silent treatment, or passive-aggressive insults. Only when cornered by a partner's attack is their suppression of attachment emotion likely to break down—which can result in an explosion of violence (see "Domestic Violence and the Avoidant" later in this book.)

Chapter 17

Distancing Life Partners

Let's look at Levine and Heller's list of distancing (deactivating) strategies again:

- Saying (or thinking) "I'm not ready to commit"—but staying together nonetheless, sometimes for years.
- Focusing on small imperfections in your partner: the way s/he talks, dresses, eats, or (fill in the blank) and allowing it to get in the way of your romantic feelings.
- Pining after an ex-girlfriend/ boyfriend—(the "phantom ex"...).
- Flirting with others—a hurtful way to introduce insecurity into the relationship.
- Not saying "I love you"—while implying that you do have feelings toward the other person.
- Pulling away when things are going well (e.g., not calling for several days after an intimate date).
- Forming relationships with an impossible future, such as with someone who is married.
- "Checking out mentally" when your partner is talking to you.
- Keeping secrets and leaving things foggy—to maintain your feeling of independence.
- Avoiding physical closeness—e.g., not wanting to share the same bed, not wanting to have sex, walking several strides ahead of your partner.[50]

In a long-term relationship, these behaviors continue to show themselves, though perhaps in less obvious ways.

- Saying (or thinking) "I'm not ready to commit"—but staying together nonetheless, sometimes for years.

Even a married avoidant is often holding back on signals of commitment. The reservations for his departure are already booked for some point in the future, not so much because he has concrete plans to use them, but because keeping his exit plan in mind reduces the stress he feels in being so close to someone who might betray him. Cautious avoidants now refuse legal marriage since it has become more clear how costly it can be to divorce, depending on the local government's family laws and family court system. Your savvy avoidant may now demand a pre-nuptial agreement cutting the financial risk in case of marriage failure. Other signs of this desire to keep escape routes open include delaying estate planning, failing to save for children's college educations, secretly communicating with exes (not because they care about them, though in time they may seem better in selective memory than their current partner), considering employment opportunities in faraway cities, or maintaining a pied-à-terre, hunting shack, or vacation cottage and visiting it alone "to take care of things." To the extent that this escape plan reduces the stress the avoidant feels in being in a relationship, you could view it as helpful; but it does show that they find the idea of leaving you not only thinkable, but something worth planning for.

- Focusing on small imperfections in your partner: the way s/he talks, dresses, eats, or (fill in the blank) and allowing it to get in the way of your romantic feelings.

The avoidant looks for reasons not to admire and feel close to their partner. This sitting in judgment over even trivial stylistic issues gives them a feeling of control; they consciously believe they are distancing themselves not because they are afraid of being dependent and hurt (the real subconscious reason), but because their partner is so flawed and really not all that great. This deprecation of a partner or spouse is normally (and wisely) kept internal, but in later stages of relationship conflict, the avoidant may start running down his partner verbally and try to get more distance by intentionally causing distress:

> We also suspect that avoidant individuals display aggression indirectly, even if they are not prone to violence. They are likely to engage in "passive aggression," which includes expressions of indifference, disrespect, and contempt, and to use violence as a means of distancing themselves from a partner who will not leave them alone. These reactions, which fit comfortably with attachment-system deactivation, can easily be perceived by a partner as psychologically abusive, which might cause the partner to react aggressively. Thus, even if not directly aggressive themselves, avoidant partners may be involved in mutually violent and abusive acts within a couple.[51]

If your relationship has reached this stage, your avoidant partner is probably already thinking of leaving. If you can get the avoidant to accept counselling and to admit that your relationship is valuable enough to try to save it (even though they tend to think you are the problem for demanding so much from them), you may still be able to stop the cycle.

- Pining after an ex-girlfriend/ boyfriend—(the "phantom ex"…).

Some psychologists believe narcissists are dismissive-avoidants taken to the extreme, and one of the habits of the narcissist is to return to victims he has been able to use in the past for support and narcissistic supply. Garden-variety avoidants also do this, to a lesser extent—they romanticize attachments from the past that may never have been very deep, but since they did not get close enough for long enough to the object of their desire to start the cycle of denigration and disrespect, they believe these distant figures are perfect and would be a good place to return to in their minds to escape present relationships with their altogether-too-real problems and demands. Your avoidant may even compare you to some idealized past figure as a way of hurting you to make you see how lucky you are to have even the limited attention they can provide.

- Flirting with others—a hurtful way to introduce insecurity into the relationship.

As with the other distancing techniques, this begins internally or secretly, but can later advance to open disrespect for your relationship by flirting meaningfully right in front of you (assuming you have a standard monogamous relationship.) This, too, is intended to remind you the avoidant is a player and has other options. The more secretive flirting and even affairs are these days more likely to occur online; it is one thing if your partner talks to you about it and reassures you it's just for fun, but another if he's secretly on online hookup sites pretending to be single or telling others that he's looking for a change in partners.

- Not saying "I love you"—while implying that you do have feelings toward the other person.

Merely saying "I love you" can become rote after awhile. If you have a long-term relationship with someone who finds it hard to say "I love you," this can mean little so long as their actions tell you they are supportive and caring and that you are really important to them. Some avoidants are able to mouth the words without feeling the feelings, and here, too, actions are more important. Buying you flowers and gifts, remembering your anniversary and birthday, and occasionally saying sweet things don't make up for inattention and an unwillingness to consider your needs as important.

- Pulling away when things are going well (e.g., not calling for several days after an intimate date).

The equivalent in a relationship is distancing behaviors right after satisfying sex, or starting to pull away after an experience that temporarily brought you closer, such as the avoidant partner's illness. The avoidant will try to regain a sense of self-sufficiency by distancing after an experience that reminds him of how much he in fact depends on the relationship.

  • Forming relationships with an impossible future, such as with someone who is married.

When in a relationship, this takes the form of affairs with others who are unavailable—often married. Fictional Dismissive Don Draper from *Mad Men* specialized in seducing attractive young women for fun, but his romantic affairs tended to be with married women, business associates, or in one case his child's teacher.

  • "Checking out mentally" when your partner is talking to you.

Like the other distancing strategies, this one gets more and more blatant as the avoidant's contempt for the partner and the relationship increases with the years. This begins as a tendency of the avoidant to switch topics back to himself, and later with a complete lack of interest in response, so either not responding or just saying "uh-huh" without actually understanding what was said.

  • Keeping secrets and leaving things foggy—to maintain your feeling of independence.

If your partner was vague about what he was doing with his time away from you while you were courting, you shouldn't expect this failure to disclose would improve after you move in together. The avoidant has walled off much of his inner state from others—including you. The idea of sharing innermost thoughts and feelings is the essence of intimacy, and exactly what scares the avoidant—by controlling information, they feel more in control of the relationship, which makes them feel safer.

> • Avoiding physical closeness—e.g., not wanting to share the same bed, not wanting to have sex, walking several strides ahead of your partner.[52]

If either or both of you snore loudly or can't sleep next to another person, the idea of sleeping apart is simply a practical accommodation. But if no such impediment exists and your avoidant wants separate bedrooms, and especially if sex is becoming a distant memory, your avoidant partner is checking out of the relationship. Not wanting to introduce you to business associates, friends, or people from other areas of his life is part of the compartmentalization they prefer—you are not presentable, and being unable to control you or what you say to others means you may embarrass him or reveal things that damage his carefully-controlled image. Normally secure people don't mind being humanized by having everyone meet their partners.

Chapter 18

Anxious-Preoccupied with Avoidant

If you are Anxious-Preoccupied yourself and have an Avoidant partner, this chapter and the next are especially for you.

Avoidants and the Anxious-Preoccupied are in a sense complementary: the Preoccupied values relationships too highly and thinks about them too much, while the Avoidant (especially the Dismissive) devalues relationships and tends not to be too concerned about them. If the Preoccupied were a bit more secure they'd be able to dial back the attention to their relationships to a healthier level that would make them happier and more successful, while if the Dismissive could only surface those attachment feelings lurking in his subconscious and value his relationships more consciously, he would also be happier and more successful.

Many of us bond to partners whose attachment style (and other characteristics) reprise dramas from the family we grew up in. It's often observed that many people end up married to people who remind them of the opposite-sex parent, and the attraction of the same psychological signalling games we used with our caregivers when we were children is that it is comforting and familiar, and confirms our sense of ourselves.

> The fact that many people find romantic excitement in a lover who displays the qualities of a rejecting parent, an excitement they do not find in others, suggest the degree to which they remain not just committed to but enthralled by early attachment figures. They can't let go of the mother or father

who didn't love them the way they needed to be loved. And they continue to be bewitched by the hurtfulness that compromised their care. They are caught in the parental orbit, a hurt child still leaning out for a love that can never be, and blinded to what they are doing by the belief they have no feelings toward their parents at all or have washed their hands of them.[53]

This is why we observe the outsize number and surprising stability (if not happiness) of Anxious-Preoccupied and Dismissive-Avoidant pairings.

The Anxious-Preoccupied would be wise to look for a Secure partner who can help build security and likely make for a happier marriage [quoting from *Bad Boyfriends*]:

The preoccupied wife who had ambivalent attachment to her parent cannot believe her husband when he says, despite their fights and mutual dissatisfactions, that he genuinely loves her and wants to stay with her. She cannot assimilate it to her worldview, her internal model. She is sure he will abandon her, either because he already wants to or because her impossible and anxious neediness will eventually drive him out. But his steadfastness over the years builds her trust. It causes her to remember her relationship with a great uncle, whose love was precious and unwavering, and to think more and more about him and how good she felt about herself around him. Gradually, she assimilates her marriage to this model, and it becomes more central. Feeling more secure, she now finds herself freer to reflect on the past.[54]

Though is appears a preoccupied person might be better off with a secure partner, some research indicates that in this case opposites attract:

A number of studies have looked into the question of whether we are attracted to people based on their attachment style or ours. Two researchers in the field of adult attachment, Paula Pietromonaco, of the University of Massachusetts, and Katherine Carnelley, of the University of Southampton in the UK, found that avoidant individuals actually prefer anxiously attached people. Another study, by Jeffry Simpson of the University of Minnesota, showed that anxious women are more likely to date avoidant men. Is it possible, then, that people who guard their independence with ferocity would seek the partners most likely to impinge on their autonomy? Or that people who seek closeness are attracted to people who want to push them away? And if so, why? Pietromonaco and Carnelley believe that these attachment styles actually complement each other in a way. Each reaffirms the other's beliefs about themselves and about relationships. The avoidants' defensive self-perception that they are strong and independent is confirmed, as is the belief that others want to pull them into more closeness than they are comfortable with. The anxious types find that their perception of wanting more intimacy than their partner can provide is confirmed, as is their anticipation of ultimately being let down by significant others. So, in a way, each style is drawn to reenact a familiar script over and over again[55].

This kind of complementary dysfunction can lead to a stable relationship, but one where both partners stay in their insecure styles, with the preoccupied battling for every scrap of attention and the avoidant one only giving enough to confirm his view of attachment as a necessary evil. These attractions are based on re-enacting the dysfunctional touch and response cycles of their early childhoods, and generally these couples report they are together despite their unhappiness.

An interesting post by Peg Streep on the *Psychology Today* blogs ("Why Your Partner May Be Like Your Parent"—see the footnote for link) goes into more depth on "replaying old family patterns:"

> Perhaps nothing is as disheartening as the discovery—after
> years of trying to escape from your dysfunctional childhood—
> that you have actually managed to recreate it. One woman, the
> daughter of a hypercritical and demanding mother, recently
> talked with me about her recently-ended, two-decades-long
> marriage: "I still have issues with feeling capable and doing
> things right. Unfortunately, I married my mother and was
> never able to feel competent in my husband's eyes, either. I also
> never really felt loved by him, in the same way I didn't feel
> loved by my mother."

> A man emailed me recently with similar concerns: "On the
> surface, my wife and my mother have nothing in common. My
> wife is petite and blonde, well-educated, polished, and
> sophisticated; my brunette and big-boned mother is none of
> those things. But they both criticize me constantly. Nothing I
> ever did was good enough for my mother because my older
> brother was perfect. My wife rules the roost with a dissatisfied
> look on her face which is depressing and familiar."

> ...A study by Glenn Geher suggests that we do tend to choose a
> romantic partner who is similar to our opposite-sex parent. In
> his research, he not only asked participants to self-report on
> how their romantic partners were like their opposite-sex
> parents across various categories—he actually interviewed the
> parents as well. The shared characteristics he discovered
> between his subjects' partners and their opposite-sex parents
> were robust, and not merely coincidental. Needless to say, when
> romantic partners were like parents in good ways, relationship
> satisfaction was high; when the similarities were related to
> negative characteristics, however, relationship satisfaction was
> low.

When we meet someone new, it's not just our unconscious models that are in the room or at the bar; there are conscious assessments, too. So the question remains: How do we end up marrying Mom if she's been critical, unavailable or unloving? That's exactly what Claudia Chloe Brumbaugh and R. Chris Fraley asked: How do insecurely attached people attract mates? After all, we all want a securely attached partner—one who's emotionally available, loving, supportive, dependable—not an insecure or clingy one, or someone who's detached and uncommunicative. How do we get roped in?

The researchers suggested that what happens is a combination of misreading by one partner and a fair amount of strategizing and even dissembling by the insecure partner. They point out that anxiously attached people may seem fascinating at first— their preoccupation with themselves may easily be confused with self-disclosure and openness, which facilitates a sense of connection. Similarly, an avoidant person may come across as independent and strong. In a series of experiments, the team discovered that avoidants—despite the fact that they don't want emotional connection—actually made lots of eye contact and used touch more than securely attached people to seem more appealing in a dating situation. Avoidants use humor in dating situations to create a sense of sharing and detract from their essential aloofness. Although the researchers didn't use Bartholomew's distinction between fearful and dismissing avoidant types, it's clear that the fearful avoidant—who both wants and fears emotional connection—would be the hardest to read and identify. Eventually, though, the leopard will show his spots.[56]

Chapter 19

Anxious-Preoccupied with Avoidant II

As we've seen, the Anxious-Preoccupied are frequently attracted to the intermittent reinforcement provided by the Avoidant, especially the apparently cool and self-sufficient Dismissive variety. This is an unhappy pairing; but who can the Anxious-Preoccupied do well with?

Anxious-preoccupied types do poorly with each other—two needy, clingy people who do manage to calm each other's insecurities exist as couples, but it's rare, and the resulting relationship is closer to unhealthy codependence; neither will be strengthened by the bond. A mildly Preoccupied person can last with a mildly Avoidant sort, but the relationship tends to be unhappy as the bond is based on the unmet neediness of the Preoccupied and the willingness of the Avoidant to accept the attention without providing emotional security.

Levine and Heller point out that the slights and intermittent reinforcement of the attractive avoidant male often trigger activation of the female attachment system—producing intrigue and sparks. So what if he only answers your text messages days later, if at all? He's hot and just hard-to-get enough that you really want him! This is the terrible mistake so many make: they meet a secure guy and it's all so drama-free that they think he's dull:

> If you are anxious, the reverse of what happens when you meet someone avoidant happens when you meet someone secure. The messages that come across from someone secure are very

honest, straightforward, and consistent. Secures are not afraid
of intimacy and know they are worthy of love. They don't have
to beat around the bush or play hard to get. Ambiguous
messages are out of the mix, as are tension and suspense. As a
result, your attachment system remains relatively calm. Because
you are used to equating an activated attachment system with
love, you conclude that this can't be "the one" because no bells
are going off. You associate a calm attachment system with
boredom and indifference. Because of this fallacy you might let
the perfect partner pass you by.[57]

So armed with foreknowledge, a wise preoccupied person will seek
out a Secure and avoid the sometimes attractive but ultimately
unsupportive Avoidant of both flavors, as well as other Preoccupieds,
who are likely to be the worst partners of all for them.

The relationships between Anxious-Preoccupied and Avoidant
partners are especially problematic, because their mutually-
reinforcing insecurities can lead to a stable but unhappy partnership
that does little to help them grow more secure but can go on for years.

Remember that while attachment types are relatively fixed
characteristics, almost everyone can display insecurities when the
situation is stressful or their partner is triggering them: as when the
Avoidant are withholding responses, creating anxiety in their partner;
or when the Anxious-Preoccupied are peppering their normally
Secure partner with demands for response, creating a desire to
distance from excessive clinginess.

The Anxious-Preoccupied are driven by their need for attachment to
jump quickly into relationships and to immediately see the latest one
as the solution to their problems:

[Of the Anxious-Preoccupied] According to Morgan and
Shaver (1999), their tendency to commit too early, often before

they know their partner very well, leaves anxious people more vulnerable to entanglement with a hurtful, uncommitted partner who frustrates their wishes for security and stability. Indeed, Hazan and Shaver (1987) found that anxious people tended to agree with the statement, "Few people are as willing and able as I am to commit themselves to a long-term relationship."[58]

They feel safe when their desired partner is near and reassuring, and anxious when apart, or when messages aren't replied to immediately. While a Secure will assume the lack of response means their partner is simply busy or away from the phone, an Anxious-Preoccupied person will start to worry and wonder if something has gone wrong with their relationship. Since they are so concerned about their relationships, they will then act—with more and increasingly demanding messages and even more obsessive worry if there is no response.

This entitled attitude ("I am a devoted partner so I am owed the attention I deserve!") leads to disappointment and anger when no real person can instantly be as thoughtful and devoted as the Preoccupied would require. The Preoccupied spend much time obsessing about these unintended slights and going over every detail of interactions in their heads, making up scenarios where they lose their partner, and then being tempted to make another play for reassurance. The anxiety they feel and the demands they make without regard to their partner's state of mind or current ability to respond ultimately can drive away partners and friends:

> [A]nxiously attached people wanted more intimacy than they were experiencing (Mikulincer & Erev, 1991). It was not clear whether anxious people were simply unable to elicit the extreme level of intimacy they desired from their partners, or whether their needy, "hungry" style of relating caused their partners to establish greater self-protective distance.[59]

The increasing percentage of Dismissives in the dating pool as time goes on means that older Preoccupieds will encounter more Dismissives than any other type. The intermittent reinforcement provided by a Dismissive—sometimes they will respond reassuringly, sometimes not—means that when the attachment system of the Preoccupied goes on alert, it finds its challenging match in the Dismissive's refusal to play along. To some Preoccupieds this partial response is what they remember from significant caregivers, most typically their father, and the familiarity of this yearning is itself attractive.

The Dismissive, on the other hand, expects partners to be too demanding and troublesome, and the Preoccupied's neediness confirms their view of others. One might expect Dismissives to seek out partners who are happy to accept greater distance in partnership, but that is not how it works out in practice; it as as if the Dismissive is most comfortable exercising the balance of power in the relationship, holding their struggling partner at a distance and just providing enough attention and reassurance to keep them on the hook.

Since they are reinforcing each other's view of others, neither will get any more secure with time; the Dismissive will accuse their partner of being clingy or needy, while the Preoccupied will accuse their partner of being too distant and uncaring. They are fulfilling each other's basic need to have a partner, but the partnership will always be troubled by their complementary insecurities. Yet it is more likely to be stable than a Preoccupied-Preoccupied partnership.

The single Preoccupied person would be wise to resist the tendency to fall for a Dismissive. This can be avoided by noting the red flags of the avoidant: not responding reassuringly to simple in-person requests, not showing much interest and concern for your feelings, and having a history of bad or no relationships. Superficial looks and accomplishments should not be seen as indicating that your new prospect is a success in emotional or relationship spheres. Always remember when you meet someone intriguing that you know next to nothing about their personality until you have seen them in many situations over many months. Don't try to have a significant relationship with someone until you have enough history with that person to be able to rely on their feelings for you. Remind yourself that there are many possible partners out there, and don't settle emotionally on someone who may not be right for you just because they have shown you a little attention. It is meaningless unless it is sustained and reliable.

Meanwhile, when paired with a Dismissive or Fearful-Avoidant, the Preoccupied push their partners into withdrawal and passive-aggressive distancing, or even to violence:

> Couples in which an anxious person is paired with an avoidant one tend to produce destructive pursuit-distancing or demand–withdrawal patterns of relating. In such couples, the anxious partner's needs and demands frustrate the avoidant partner's preference for distance, and the avoidant partner's tendency to create distance frustrates the anxious partner's intense desire for closeness. As a result, both partners are dissatisfied and can become abusive or violent when attempting to influence their partner's undesirable behavior.[60]

A big meta-analysis of 74 studies, including more than 14,000 participants, was written up as "A Meta-Analytical Review of the Demand/Withdraw Pattern of Interaction and its Associations with Individual, Relational, and Communicative Outcomes," and published in *Communication Monographs* (March, 2014).

The studies cover what happens to relationships where the Preoccupied partner makes increasing demands for reassurance, while the Dismissive partner fails to respond, either deflecting/avoiding or going silent—the "silent treatment."

"It's the most common pattern of conflict in marriage or any committed, established romantic relationship," says Paul Schrodt, Ph.D., professor and graduate director of communication studies at Texas Christian University. "And it does tremendous damage."

Schrodt led a meta-analysis of 74 studies, including more than 14,000 participants, "A Meta-Analytical Review of the Demand/Withdraw Pattern of Interaction and its Associations with Individual, Relational, and Communicative Outcomes," published in Communication Monographs (March, 2014).

Research shows couples engaged in demand-withdraw pattern experience lower relationship satisfaction, less intimacy and poorer communication. The damage can be emotional and physical; the presence of demand-withdraw pattern is associated with anxiety and aggression as well as physiological effects (urinary, bowel or erectile dysfunction). It's also a very hard pattern to break.

"Partners get locked in this pattern, largely because they each see the other as the cause," says Schrodt. "Both partners see the other as the problem." Ask the wife—whom research shows is more often the demanding partner—and she'll complain that her husband is closed off, emotionally unavailable. Ask the husband and he'll say he might open up if she'd just back off. Regardless of the role each partner plays, the outcome is equally distressing. "One of the most important things we found is that even though wife-demand/husband-withdraw occurs more frequently, it's not more or less damaging," he says. No matter what part each partner plays, it's the pattern itself that's the problem. "It's a real, serious sign of distress in the relationship."[61]

See the *hyperactivation* pattern in chapter 2, "Touch and Response." The Anxious-Preoccupied will remain in this stressful pattern for much longer than a more secure person, who would start to move to the *attachment-avoidance* strategy, hastening a breakup of the relationship. This is how these relationships last despite the stress and negative consequences for both partners, who are unable to break out of the pattern.

> Anxious people's desire for closeness and worries about rejection and unlovability seem to favor more intense, possessive, and dependent kinds of love (e.g., mania). J. A. Feeney and Noller (1990) and Sperling and Berman (1991) provided further support for this view: Attachment anxiety was associated with higher scores on scales tapping love addiction, "limerence" (Tennov, 1979), and desperate love. This desperate need for love may explain A. Aron, Aron, and Allen's (1998) finding of more frequent unreciprocated love among people with an anxious attachment style.[62]

> [A]nxious adults' overdependence on relationship partners, fears of abandonment and separation, and doubts about their ability to handle life challenges alone lead them to maintain relationships at all costs, even if it implies staying in an unhappy marriage. (Later, in the section dealing with relationship violence, we discuss similar findings concerning anxious adults' difficulties in leaving a violent relationship). According to Davila and Bradbury, spouses' attachment anxiety "may make them unhappy in their marriage and at the same time keep them in their marriage. Hence, the stability of such marriages may be grounded in insecurity rather than satisfaction."[63]

> Anxious individuals are also vulnerable to dissatisfaction, but they seem more likely to deal with it by staying in an unfulfilling relationship, unless their partners leave them.

Perhaps to them, being alone seems even less likely to be fulfilling than sticking with a struggling relationship. As we will see, this reluctance to leave makes anxious adults vulnerable to psychological and physical abuse. Secure individuals can stay with a committed long-term relationship when problems can be resolved, but they also have the self-confidence and perhaps supportive social network to help them successfully leave a dangerous or persistently dissatisfying relationship.[64]

It's important to note both partners are capable of adjusting their communication styles to make their relationship more satisfying to both; while it is harder for the Dismissive, who often don't see a reason to change, they can learn to respond reassuringly more often. Discussion of the problem can help, especially if the Anxious-Preoccupied partner learns to rely more on inner assurance and reduce the rate and insistence of messages requesting reassurance. This makes both partners more comfortable:

> Avoidant people's preference for interpersonal distance was expected to interfere with both their own intimacy-promoting behavior and their responsiveness to a partner's bids for proximity and intimacy. Anxious people's unmet needs for closeness were expected to cause them to seek closeness to such an extent that it would make their partners uncomfortable. Moreover, fear of rejection was expected to cause them to misinterpret a partner's desire for privacy or autonomy as a sign of rejection, which could tempt them to escalate demands for intimacy to such an extent that, paradoxically, it might cause their partner to withdraw or flee. Pistole noted that this kind of intrusion would be most unwelcome to avoidant partners, who view even normal intimacy and proximity as intrusive. This relational pattern , which in the marital research literature is called "demand-withdrawal" (Christensen, 1988) or "pursuit-withdrawal" (Bartholomew & Allison, 2006), is one of the major predictors of relationship violence and distress.[65]

Chapter 20

Serial Monogamy

Avoidants need intimacy as much as anyone—but the Dismissive have convinced themselves they really don't, while the Fearful-Avoidant will seek it out and then go into an approach-avoidance pattern where the desired intimacy gets too frightening, compelling distancing for relief of the anxiety produced by fear of abandonment. Both types of Avoidants can be part of stable but generally unhappy relationships when they find someone whose anxieties dovetail—who is willing to do all of the emotional fixing work to keep the relationship going, with the most common enabler being the Anxious-Preoccupied type living in a state of anxiety from the inconsistent support she gets from her partner.

Both avoidant types are more likely to be in unsatisfying relationships, with the Fearful-Avoidant the quickest to end a marriage or relationship. Here's an example of a Fearful-Avoidant who practices rapid relationship turnover—the case of Nate:

Nate's operating mode is serial monogamy. He feels more secure with one other person and the underlying compulsion to find a source for sex and companionship compels him to try to find a monogamous LTR — over and over and over, with a breakup on average just a few months after committing.

Serial monogamy is now the dominant model for relationships in the West. Where true monogamy implies coupling for life, serial monogamy is exclusive only for a limited time, and implies that when an exclusive relationship stops working for the benefit of either partner, it should end and new partners be found. The old model of forever-after monogamy is honored mostly in the breach, still held up as an ideal though longer lives, urban surroundings, and increased wealth reduced the benefits and increased the opportunity cost of permanent commitments. Even politicians can't conform to the permanent monogamy standard, it seems, though for the benefit of voters they continue to talk about it in glowing terms.

Younger people in the upper classes now mostly accept the more realistic expectation that they will have multiple partners in their lifetimes. An article from *The Dartmouth Free Press* (no longer available online) expressed the modern view, excerpted here:

> Serial monogamists are undoubtedly looking for love, admiration, and respect, but find themselves in mismatched relationships, until (they pray) one will end the series. If you are in such a situation, consider the compromises and sacrifices outlined in the tongue-in-cheek book *Does He Love Me or Am I Just Paranoid? The Serial Monogamist's Guide to Love* by Carina Chocano: "Step 1: Lower Your Standards. Start by asking yourself the following: Does he really have to be attractive? Does he really have to be smart? Does he really have to be clean? Does he really have to be sane? Step 2: Question Your Instincts. Your gut is telling you to run far away. Pretend not to hear it....Step 3: Accentuate the Positive. Before dismissing someone as "ugly" or "crazy," take the time to examine his positive qualities: Is he wonderfully weird? Is he thrillingly obsessive-compulsive? Is he expertly medicated?"

So Nate is not alone in this seemingly fruitless emphasis on an outcome that never happens for him over the acceptance and enjoyment of flawed partners as they are, while in the process of getting to know them. The unusual aspect of Nate's relationship history is the number of partners he's tried out and the speed of the breakups; otherwise he's in the mainstream. Family and friends and society at large have told him he should try to achieve permanent partnership with someone respectable, and in pursuit of that goal he will break and leave behind any relationship that doesn't seem to be heading in that direction, usually because he becomes aware that his prospective partner will end up boring him in time. This is a problem for all really smart people; finding someone who will be stimulating for a lifetime is very much harder than it is for more normal people.

Nate's prospective partners have mostly been of the same mindset: seeking stability and permanence, and often devastated when such a seemingly perfect boyfriend dumps them. Nate has not helped them much by tending to go along with their plans at first; he has not learned the trick of reducing expectations and being forthcoming about the tentative nature of his interest, so until recently they have had good reason to feel let down when he exited abruptly under the pressure of their expectations. But they, too, only see one brass ring to try for, and reject a relationship that might be satisfying and worthwhile even if not leading to their ideal outcome. And so everyone who lives this dominant paradigm is set up for disappointment and loss while surrounded by interesting and attractive people who'd want to spend time with them....

Chapter 21

Domestic Violence and the Avoidant

Research shows that avoidants generally are not much more likely to be physically abusive than others, though it does appear the fearful-avoidant (also called anxious-avoidant, because they are insecure about themselves) have a greater tendency to lash out. Dismissives especially, though, will resort to passive-aggressive insults and distancing when they feel pressured to respond, and if pushed hard enough they can become explosively and violently angry. This is most common when their partner is anxious-preoccupied and doesn't realize that constant pushing for attention simply makes the avoidant more and more uncomfortable.

As I write this (September of 2014), the news channels are spending a lot of time on football star Ray Rice's abuse of his then-fiancée Janay in a shocking video—as they enter an elevator, there is an argument, Janay lunges at Ray, and Ray punches her hard enough to knock her off her feet so that her head hits a grab bar and knocks her out.

This domestic assault is indefensible, but part of a complex dynamic —not just "bad man, innocent woman," but "couple in deep trouble." Careful research is showing that domestic violence against men is almost as prevalent as against women, though men rarely report it and authorities tend to assume the man is the perpetrator when there is violence. Some forms of domestic violence are actually about control—with the abuser keeping the abused in terror and knocking the victim around to punish perceived transgressions against that control. Other domestic violence is more like violent versions of the fights many couples have—with aggression and counter-aggression escalating to assault, both parties assaulting each other. In those cases it is not especially helpful to call one party the "victim."

Janay is now coming to Ray's defense and telling us he's a good man who had a bad moment. This may even be true. I'm guessing Janay's anger flared and she said something ugly and lunged at Ray before he punched her, and she probably feels guilty for her part in setting up the situation (and has said as much)—though of course the punch was beyond a reasonable response.

Over at the *Just Four Guys* blog, writer Obsidian points out some inconsistencies between how this incident—which for now seems to have ended Ray's career in football—and a similar recent incident where a woman was the assailant:

> Astute watchers of current events will have noticed however, that another event that took place on an elevator, the smoking gun footage of which was also released by TMZ and which also took place earlier this year, was treated in a completely different manner than the current Rice issue is being handled. In that instance, Ms. Solange Knowles, kid sister to pop icon Beyoncé Knowles, viciously attacked Bey's hubbie, rap mogul Jay-Z, barely restrained by a burly bodyguard. Right there on the tape, we see Solange trying to kick Jay-Z, throw punches and the like, while he remained cool and calm, and even tried to restrain Ms. Knowles, again, assisted by the aforementioned burly bodyguard.

> While Mr. Rice's career, for the time being at least, lay in tatters, Ms. Knowles not only didn't get so much as a slap on the wrist for her clearly violent actions, there were people who openly speculated what Jigga "could have done" to PROVOKE such a visceral response on the part of Solange—the same people, in fact, who now ride high in their saddles, finger wagging at Mr. Rice. Clearly, suggesting that Women could provoke a

beatdown is worthy of being censured, even fired; but suggesting that a Man could have provoked a Woman into going into full-on Mighty Joe Young mode, well, that's perfectly A-OK.

For anyone out there who agrees with the punishment Mr. Rice has received for his actions on that fateful Winter night earlier this year, you are a stompdown hypocrite with a capital "H" if you do not also support the full-on blacklisting of Mr. Solange Knowles from the music and entertainment business - but, of course, like Ms. Mary J. Blige before her, Ms. Knowles will go on with her life as if nothing had ever happened, continuing to ply her trade as a singer/entertainer, making a nice bit of coin for herself. Because, only Women count when it comes to domestic violence or spousal abuse.[66]

Because women are on average smaller and less strong, and lingering notions of chivalry have them as the gentler sex, many people (and the laws) still assume men are the perpetrators. Yet we know that this is not always so—while women's assaults tend to be less forceful, screaming, slapping, punching, and clawing at your husband's face is not stereotypically gentle, feminine behavior. And large numbers of men are, in fact, assaulted and controlled by their wives in this manner, but get almost no sympathy or help from law enforcement when they (foolishly, as it turns out) try to report it.

What we can say about these kinds of fights is that it is difficult for outsiders to tell from one incident exactly how the dynamics of the couple evolved to that point. In some cases the aggressor (often a malignant narcissist) is simply lashing out to control his/her partner; in other cases both partners have been assaulting each other regularly, verbally if not physically, for some time, building up anger. And this is often a case where an Anxious-Preoccupied woman has been escalating her demands for response, building up anger in a Dismissive-Avoidant or Fearful-Avoidant mate who *just wants it to stop.* I'm going to speculate that they are an Anxious-Preoccupied / Avoidant couple, and use this now-famous incident to discuss the dynamic of those couples.

Secure couples generally communicate well and never get to this endpoint of conflict and tit-for-tat, which is one reason why their relationships tend to be happier and last longer.

There have been some studies of attachment type's relationship to domestic violence; these tend to show the Anxious-Preoccupied as the more likely instigators:

> In light of this theoretical analysis, it is easy to understand why anxious adults, who are chronically afraid of rejection and separation, and are often pessimistic about the future of their relationships, are inclined to perpetrate acts of violence against a romantic partner. These destructive acts of protest can be further intensified by anxious individuals' difficulties in managing anger and their ineffective communication of strong needs for love and attention. As a result, they are more likely than secure individuals to strike out aggressively as a means of gaining or regaining proximity to their partner during couple disagreements and conflicts.[67]

Typically Dismissive-Avoidants minimize emotional conflict and avoid arguments and scenes by using deactivating strategies: withdrawal, avoiding intimacy or discussion of problems. But when an Anxious-Preoccupied partner is using escalating protest behaviors, the Dismissive may be driven beyond his ability to distance, and lose the control they usually strive for; a shocking explosion of anger may be the result.

What little research there is on this relationship pattern suggests it may explain many of the domestic violence incidents between the Anxious-Preoccupied and the Avoidant:

Some attachment researchers have suggested that avoidant individuals are also more likely than their secure counterparts to engage in acts of violence during couple conflicts because of their hostility, narcissism, and dysfunctional approach to conflict management. However, Bartholomew and Allison (2006) reasoned that avoidant people's tendency to withdraw from interpersonal conflicts and suppress overt expressions of anger and hostility might actually discourage outright aggression toward a relationship partner. Even Bartholomew and Allison mention, however, that avoidant people can become violent when involved in negative reciprocity and a demand-withdrawal behavioral dynamic with a partner (who is likely to be anxiously attached). They give a harrowing example from one of their studies in which a man refused to keep arguing with his wife after they had been up most of the night fighting (he was trying to relax with a newspaper before leaving for work). His anxious partner stabbed him in the back with a kitchen knife, which definitely got his attention and caused him to become enraged in return. Bartholomew and Allison point out that the correlation between one partner being violent and the other partner also being violent is above .60 in most studies of couple violence, which suggests that people with violent tendencies either choose one another as mates, or that one partner's violence provokes the other partner's violence in turn. Probably both causal pathways exist; that is, if there is reciprocity of negative affect in a couple and/or a demand-withdrawal pattern in their interactions, the partners may mutually goad each other to become more abusive. We also suspect that avoidant individuals display aggression indirectly, even if they are not prone to violence. They are likely to engage in "passive aggression," which includes expressions of indifference, disrespect, and contempt, and to use violence as a means of distancing themselves from a partner who will not leave them alone. These reactions, which fit comfortably with attachment-system deactivation, can easily be perceived by a partner as psychologically abusive, which might cause the partner to react aggressively. Thus, even if not directly aggressive themselves, avoidant partners may be involved in mutually violent and abusive acts within a couple.[68]

Now with the public attitudes we have and the law enforcement tilt toward assuming the male is the aggressor, it may well be that many of the men accused of domestic violence are Avoidant (of either type) who have simply been unable to defuse a bad situation by responding soothingly to escalating demands from an Anxious-Preoccupied partner, and lashed out as only the last step in a long conflict.

Is there any evidence that might show this? Some:

With regard to avoidant attachment, most of the studies... did not turn up significant associations with relationship violence. However, Holtzworth-Munroe et al. found that avoidance was significantly higher among battering men than among nondistressed men, and Rankin, Saunders, and Williams found that higher avoidance in a sample of African American men who had been arrested for partner abuse was associated with perpetration of more frequent and severe acts of abuse toward romantic partners. In addition, more than one-third of the studies that assessed the link between attachment style and violence in unrestricted samples of adolescents and young adults found that men and women who scored higher on avoidance reported higher levels of violence against romantic partners. This kind of association has been found even prospectively, when avoidance was assessed during adolescence and perpetration of violence was assessed 6 years later (Collins et al., 2002).... we conclude that when fearful and dismissing forms of avoidance were distinguished, only fearful avoidance was related to violence. Thus, the few associations with avoidance might actually be due to fearful avoidance, which is a combination of anxiety and avoidance. If this is correct, it suggests that anxiety is the major culprit in facilitating violence.[69]

And the Anxious-Preoccupied partner will have trouble ending a relationship even after abuse; their tendency to put up with bad marriages out of fear of never finding another is one of the reasons that the numerous Anxious-Preoccupied/Avoidant marriages last a surprisingly long time despite mutual unhappiness. So Janay's desire to forgive, forget, and move on is not uncommon, and may be based on more than a desire to continue to enjoy the benefits of marriage to a football star.

Mikulincer and Shaver have something to say about the research on this:

> [G]iven the previously mentioned mutuality of violence, most of the victims are also perpetrators. Therefore, logically, the same variables have to predict both perpetration and victimization. Longitudinal studies indicate that abused women who previously scored higher on attachment anxiety had more problems in resolving their feelings of separation 6 months after leaving their romantic partner. For example, they engaged in more frequent sexual contact and emotional involvement with their old partner after separation (Henderson, Bartholomew, & Dutton, 1997; see also D. Davis et al., 2003). This finding fits with Davila and Bradbury's (2001) conclusion that anxious people are unable or unwilling to leave unhappy relationships. More important, it suggests that such people may form a "traumatic bond" with an abusive partner that puts them at risk for further abuse.[70]

Chapter 22

Sex and the Avoidant

Dismissive-Avoidants (like everyone else) like sex, and since they are generally not as interested in long-term attachment, they pursue relationships for the sex more than most people, and assume new relationships won't last as long. Fearful-Avoidants are definitely interested in the idea of a long-term attachment, but also know from past experience that most of their relationships don't last, so they too make sexual attraction a prime motivation for seeking out companionship.

> Avoidant people's discomfort with closeness and negative models of others may interfere with psychological intimacy and interpersonal sensitivity in sexual situations. In addition, avoidant people may be willing to engage in sex without any consideration of establishing a long-term relationship, or even with the conviction that they do not want to be burdened by a long-term relationship. In other words, avoidance may be associated with measurable erotophobia (i.e., fearing or backing away from sex), sexual abstinence, or preference for impersonal, uncommitted sex.[71]

Some Avoidants, like everyone, have absorbed the Fairy Tale model of romance, and they often have a hazy idea that someday they will meet their "soulmate" and find true relationship happiness; in the meantime they are just getting their needs met. But more commonly they think of romantic ideals as traps for the unwary and purely fictional:

Avoidant people's preference for interpersonal distance and emotional detachment favors viewing sex and love as quite distinct; indeed, in the first studies of avoidance within the adult close-relationship domain, Hazan and Shaver (1987) found that avoidant people tended to view romantic love as a Hollywood fiction that does not exist in real life.[72]

Dismissive males often appear to be "alpha" males, since they are less concerned about how others feel, which can look like confidence and authority to someone who doesn't know them well. Many Anxious-Preoccupied women encounter these pseudo-Alphas and are smitten —they see a confident, dominant man who doesn't care too much about being responsive, and that excites their sexual and attachment system. Going after one of these men, they may have the misfortune of catching one, only to discover after a year or two together that he is not loyal and will not "protect" them, in fact may start in with passive-aggressive or even violent abuse when he feels too pushed for responsiveness he cannot give. We saw an example of this in the last chapter about Ray and Janay Rice.

[B]ecause avoidant strategies are associated with extreme self-reliance, personal control, and defensive self-image inflation... avoidant people may use sex to maximize control over a partner, to gain social prestige, or to enhance self-esteem, all without much regard for a partner's feelings. In fact, avoidant people's sexual behavior may be focused selfishly on their own needs in combination with dismissal of or blindness to a partner's sexual wishes. Avoidance also, paradoxically, may promote sexual promiscuity powered by insecurity, narcissism, or a wish to elevate one's self-image or standing in the estimation of one's peers. This kind of self-promotion through sexual conquest can occur in the absence of intense sexual interest and without much enjoyment of sex per se.[73]

Avoidants may be extremely accomplished at sex—the more

successful of them may have had hundreds of partners and learned much more about sex with a wider variety of people than those who are secure and have few but deeper relationships. Avoidants are more likely to cheat on current partners as well, but experience does pay off in technique.

> Beyond abstaining from sex, avoidant individuals seem to construe sexual activities in ways that make intimacy and interdependence unlikely. Several studies that have assessed attitudes toward casual sex (e.g., acceptance of casual sex without love, acceptance of uncommitted sex) found that avoidant attachment is associated with more positive attitudes toward casual sex....[74]

It is not unusual for an avoidant to deny their current partner affection and sex while at the same time chasing after outside sexual partners and pursuing secretive sex lives away from home. But if they're not in a relationship, they will typically be more interested in sex that will not draw them into the intimacy of a real relationship.

I'll let "Greta" tell her story in correspondence about a relationship with an attractive fearful-avoidant man:

Greta:

I am seeing a fearful-avoidant (just friends) after dating him and he unfortunately has VERY low self esteem, thinks he's not good enough for me and that I will leave him, nothing I could say or do could change that. He is subconsciously determined to let the self-fulfilling prophecy do its job and so he acts like a jerk; VERY stingy, closed off and mistrusting. But I can see his wonderfulness shining through, in a way that makes him unique, that is the other side of this emotional rollercoaster. It's all VERY confusing. Sorry for my English, I am German.

Jeb:

The distinction between fearful and dismissive is usually that the fearful are conscious of a need to attach and have low self-esteem, so are afraid of losing attachment when actual intimacy threatens. The dismissive appear to have high self-esteem and not to care very much about attachment. Usually dismissives end up in relationships seemingly by accident when they meet someone who is motivated to attach to them and they acquiesce; though of course they subconsciously want to be wanted. Both fearful and dismissive types have shorter relationships than average, but the fearful type is more likely to end one out of fear.

Your task, if you want a good relationship with this man, is to convince his subconscious that you are reliable and won't hurt him. It sounds like you cherish some things about him, and if you can talk about his fears, remind him that you feel that. If you can bring him to be conscious of his distancing and how it arises from fear of intimacy, he may be able to control it consciously. Getting an avoidant to that point can be very difficult since they generally can't detach from themselves to objectively view their behavior.

Greta:

...Wow, you're describing him like he is... almost 100%. I would love to try to get him to see his behavior and fears underneath. But it is going to be difficult. His father is a narcissist, bordering psychopath, who told him over and over that he wasn't good enough. His mother was also abused with words by his father but only left when it was too late for him and never protected him or showed a lot of love for her children.

I forgot to tell you that he never said to me directly that he fears that I will leave (he is very closed off on these topics unfortunately), but I suspect that he does, because he did say that he doesn't understand that I want to be with him. Although he pursued me at the beginning, our relationship brought unease to him, because before me he had come to terms with the idea that he would grow old alone (he is 47, I am 42), and after the thrill of the chase of me he wanted to get rid of the unease and get back to the unhappy but relatively easeful situation of being alone (that's my perspective on it now). That's why after a year he broke up with me.

But after the breakup, he wanted to keep seeing me straight away (and have a friends with benefits type of relationship, what he told me later), but I wanted a no contact period of 3 months, and since then we've been just friends, for 4 months now, and we don't see each other a lot, he wants to see me more but never calls, and is happy when I call to invite him to go out biking together for instance. At first, I wanted him to call and pursue me again, as he was the dumper and I am the dumpee, and he's the man, but I think he has a fear of calling and emailing as well, and now I can live with this situation, I don't let it consume me like it did in the beginning, and we're just friends. The sexual attraction between us is immense though, so it's difficult, haha, but it's better this way.

He likes me to be very confident with myself, he is attracted by that, which is great, but he doesn't understand that his old nit-picking and emotional stingy behavior wasn't helping (not anymore though, this was during the relationship, before I knew what was going on with him, AND at the same time he's a little bit nicer to me now). I know now that he doesn't see his part in my past insecurity because he thinks he is meaningless, so his actions are also meaningless for my self-confidence, in his logic.

He can easily talk with me about other women that he likes, but who are way beyond his level, like me, he says and who he will never get, he implies. He was and is very surprised that he got me. It's not nice, to say the least, I feel very replaceable, but at the same time I know that this won't happen very soon. But we're not bonding very strongly, to say the least. To protect myself I am approaching him now very differently; as a friend, with more humor, and a more carefree attitude, (although I always gave him space) also teasing him a bit, and now I see more admiration in his eyes, which I like, because I admire him as well; he takes care of things right away, a doer, which I would like to be more, I am more of a thinker. And he is very masculine and tender at the same time. both in- and outside the bedroom. And interested in psychology. In the near future I guess it is better to date other people, but I think I will always have a soft spot for the man, and I haven't given up on him just yet.

Jeb:

So you clearly have a spark and feeling for this man, who is emotionally crippled by abuse and the resulting low self-esteem. His pattern of responsiveness at times followed by distancing is very typical, as well as the characteristic fearful-avoidant feeling of stress when a relationship is starting to get close, followed by relief when he breaks it off. And "can't we keep having sex?" This is a very common pattern.

You're both getting to be of a certain age where just finding someone you enjoy spending some time with is good, even if it's not the long term relationship of your dreams. Realizing that he's a bit handicapped in relationships, you should probably get over the natural feeling that he should work a bit harder to take the initiative and approach him as often as you feel like seeing him. If I were you I would stay open to friendship or more with him, while at the same time seeing who out there might be a closer and more comfortable partner. He may grow into a more reliable partner, or not; you may find someone a lot easier to be with, or not. If you can be patient, something good will happen.... And unless you have another interesting man available for outings, you will at least have something to do.

Greta:

Thank you again Jeb, this helps me a lot. One last question, I hope you don't mind; do you think it's better to bond more with him (if possible) before being sexual with him again, in order to get a better and committed relationship, or can sex help guys like him bond and commit, so that he feels more masculine and strong through the sex, but less uneasy about being in a relationship because it's FWB, what he wants? And that he can grow into something more? Or would he think less of me? I hope I don't sound awful or stupid when I say that I kind of consider a FWB type of relationship with him. The sex is the best I ever had and ever will have.

But in the long term it's more important to me to mentally feel 100% good around my man (him or if that's not possible, someone else) and have him to commit to wanting to make me feel good, like I am committed to wanting him to feel good with me.

I am aware that it could make me feel vulnerable again, and I will be careful about that, but that's besides the question for now. I am wondering about the potential effect on him, of course I could always stop it again, but I am curious what you as an expert would think. Or should I get him to see his unconscious patterns before that can happen?

Jeb:

Sex—ah, there's a big problem. For some of these guys regular sex primes them to see you as only a source for sex, and when they find novelty elsewhere they move on. If you two actually have a kind of bond now (as it appears), I would personally try to make your relationship about enjoying time and activities together, with maybe occasional sex as something that happens, but not as a routine. Being an expected FWB slots you and might make him less anxious, but might also end the relationship after the sex is routine. So make sure it doesn't become routine. And using the most important bonding glue there is (sex) when the relationship itself is uncertain is likely to make you feel less secure and wanting more from him, more quickly, which would be bad for you and probably scare him. Your instincts about good partnership are dead on—he should be committed to being there for you, and vice-versa.

Greta:

Thanks for your honest, open minded and balanced response. To be honest, I was a little embarrassed for asking about this topic. I am now away from the city where we live, for three weeks, and have come to think about it the same way as you. It makes a lot of sense. Also, I would really like to see him wanting me more, I know he does, but he should show it more, like he used to do in the very beginning. But his mentality lately is to just give up on things, even things that matter to him. It originates with his lack of self esteem, unfortunately. So he shows he wants me only just before trying to make out with me. And I should not give in.

It is a really strange paradox to me sometimes, since he really made me euphoric when we got erotic in the past, he showed very strong masculine behavior. Swept me off my feet, so to speak. I really have to try to continue to withstand that, also if and when we meet at his or my place (at the moment we meet up only in public places) it will be difficult.

Also, I will try to use more humor during our meetups. And to be bubbly and positive and continue to not expect much, like I do now for a while and just take things very slowly. And date others as well and tell him in a non threatening way.

"Greta" is an unusually sensitive Secure woman trying to deal with a man who is attractive, sexy, and interesting to her, but whose fearful-avoidant attachment type is an obstacle. He is not secure enough to believe she will stay interested in him, but her secure sense of her own value enabled her to cope well with being dumped by him (which is the usual way a fearful-avoidant deals with a relationship beginning to get serious.) She is interested enough and cares enough for him to keep trying, though, which is admirable; there is a chance that with time he will begin to trust her interest in him enough to start reciprocating to build a longer-term commitment. But that is unlikely, and as I advised her, she should plan to look elsewhere for a real commitment while keeping some ties with this man.

And this example points out how avoidants treat sex—they are more capable than most of enjoying sex (which they need) without intimacy (which scares them.) If you are a more attachment-oriented person for whom sex is a bonding event, you will find getting involved in regular sex with an avoidant will only increase your feelings for the avoidant, who may not be in any shape to return those feelings; and in so doing you may end up increasing your own pain when the avoidant runs away from you because you have become more attached to them.

Chapter 23

The Runaway Avoidant

Sometimes it's better when an avoidant lets you know *before* you get into a years-long relationship that you really aren't that important to them. Painful as that might be, it's less painful than having built a life or family with them, only to discover they are just tolerating you.

Here's an example (which also demonstrates that attachment types issues are similar in gay and lesbian relationships.) "Tess" is just out of a bad romance with an avoidant ("Natasha"), and she's still trying to understand what happened:

Tess:

I am very recently out of a relationship where I think now that my former dating partner may be an avoidant, but I am not totally sure which type. I know from therapy that I'm anxious-preoccupied and I'm working on that, but this relationship activated my attachment issues. I did better this time than I have in the past, but it is still really hard.

I met this woman through work, and we hit it off and became friends. Over the course of our friendship, I developed an attraction to her, and I thought she did to me as well. Before we started she had doubts about me as I had never been with a woman before, and I had doubts as to whether or not she was over her ex.

I should have paid closer attention to was her mentioning that she was planning to move 5 hours away when she was able to find a job in that area. The only area she was willing to look for a job was in the city where her ex lives. I asked her once why the only place in the whole world she wanted to move was that close to her ex, and she responded by asking me why it bothered me.

When "Natasha" (my ex) met the woman who would become her ex, she was married and had small children. They began an affair, and eventually this woman left her husband for Natasha. They were together in some capacity for 3 years until the ex-husband threatened to take the children away if they didn't end their relationship. She ended the relationship with Natasha and moved with her ex-husband to the area where Natasha has now moved.

She also has a history of having long distance relationships that I knew about when we started dating. I really thought I wasn't jumping into anything too fast this time because we had been friends for over a year at the time we started dating. She really pursued me at the start and was very romantic. Then it was like as soon as I was in, she started distancing herself a little. I know that I am sensitive to distance because I am preoccupied, so I tried to rely on my tools I had developed and ignored my feelings. But sometimes they were overwhelming, and I would need to ask for reassurance. She always gave it and assured me that the distance was due to stress and nothing more.

She ended up moving 5 hours away for a job, and she insisted that she wanted to try long distance. I am also job searching, and so I suggested that I search for jobs in her city. She said that I should do whatever is best for me. And I said that I feel like for our relationship to move forward, we need to be in the same city. She said she agreed, but she was fine with long distance also.

I visited her after she moved, and everything seemed fine. The next day she broke up with me over the phone when I had returned home. Basically, the only answer she had was that I wasn't "The One." She still hopes we can be friends.

This break up was totally devoid of emotion. Then I called her two weeks later to talk because I missed her and just wanted to talk to her. She acted fine. She was cold and callous. She had absolutely no emotion whatsoever. Which over the course of our relationship, she didn't show a lot of emotion anyway except when she was trying to win me over it felt like.

The only time I heard a hint of emotion in her voice was when I asked about her mother. She had an edge of anger. Not much, but some.

Her father committed suicide when she was 12, and I know she doesn't have a lot of close friends. She does have a close relationship with her mother and her sister.

I am looking for answers to help myself move on…

Jeb:

She sounds primarily dismissive; most of the signs (often cold, valuing an unobtainable ex over a real available person, breaking up right after a visit) fit. Talking about moving away while seeing you is another typical sign. If she were fearful, she would have run away after really being a relationship, as it started to get very close. But the fearful and dismissive share common characteristics and some people straddle the line.

You already know she's not reliable or consistently valuing your feelings. The best thing for you is probably to move on. She sounds like she has more issues than just being avoidant, so perhaps it's just as well you didn't get in as deep as you could have. Talking about moving far away—which happens to be to a place near your ex!—while you are supposedly getting into a relationship with someone is as red-flaggy as it gets.

Tess:

Is it typical for an avoidant to act very interested in a relationship at the beginning? One of the things I am having a hard time reconciling is the fact that Natasha seemed very, very interested at the beginning, and it changed sort of suddenly. Like one day she was all about me, and then it was like she wasn't there. We still went on dates and saw each other regularly until she moved, but she seemed emotionally distant.

I asked her how her feelings changed so quickly, and she just said that her feelings haven't changed. She still thinks I am an amazing woman, but that I am just not "The One." I know from previous conversations that she had felt like her ex was "The One," but since they weren't together anymore, she was trying to believe there could be someone else.

Was she lying in the beginning about how attracted to me she was? That is one of the mental obstacles I am facing in working through this. How does a person have strong attraction and then no attraction over the course of 4 months?

Jeb:

"Lying" is probably the wrong word. Most people are aware of their motives for doing things, but the avoidant's lack of emotional connection to memories allows for an inconsistency of feeling that is hard for us to understand. A typical person would recognize something odd about wanting someone one day, then shortly thereafter rejecting the same person, but they are not conscious of a remembered "landscape of feelings" like we are.

You would not do that. But she could, and without ever lying— she could only have been lying if she wasn't truly interested, but most likely she was. No, it does not make sense. Just realize you can't fit her actions into your emotional reasoning.

It's not at all unusual for an avoidant to be charming and very interested-seeming in courtship. Avoidants can enjoy the thrill of the chase, hunt, and capture; most of the "players" (charming seducers) over 30 are avoidant. They will focus attention on you —one study found that avoidants touched their dating partners during conversation more than secure and preoccupied types. But once the prey is bagged, the level of interest drops.

Generally the dismissive aren't conscious of why they act this way; a rationalization is made up to explain their own behavior.

Chapter 24

Passive-Aggressive Abuse

As a relationship ages and the avoidant grows tired of (what they see as) unreasonable demands for support, the avoidant may resort to deprecating his partner and passive-aggressive abuse through verbal expressions of indifference and contempt.

The avoidant thinks of himself as self-contained, logical, and fair; so this expression of simmering anger takes an indirect form, not directly saying "you're making me angry with your constant demands," but subtly or not-so-subtly blaming you for being so weak as to need support.

The first and most common form of passive-aggression is withdrawal —physically leaving or mentally checking out of a conversation to avoid an emotional response. Rather than have a conversation where his feelings might come out and create further demands that he disclose, he'll avoid discussion entirely. Early in the relationship, there will be a pretext—a pressing matter he must attend to, a need to pass water, a friend he sees across the room. Later he may just leave without explanation or stop responding entirely without moving an inch; the "silent treatment."

Another form of passive-aggressive abuse is withholding sex and affection to punish a partner for making other demands; the avoidant may acquiesce to a social plan or project that the spouse believes will be fun and bring them together, then take it out on the spouse by refusing to snuggle or make love that evening, with the underlying thought being "I gave enough today." The avoidant will claim to be tired or ill, but really wants to restore a sense of independence by refusing a partner's requests. This gives the avoidant that sense of controlling the depth of the relationship they require to feel safe.

Less obvious forms of passive-aggressive behavior are often deniable as single incidents, but build up to a pattern of subconscious intent over time. Examples of this are conveniently forgetting appointments and requests you have made, commenting ambiguously in a way that could be seen as insulting but might not be ("wow, your sister is really taking good care of herself. I wonder what she's doing?" with the unspoken "...that you're not?") If you have something important you want to do, the passive-aggressive avoidant will often seem to be cooperating, but somehow never gets around to doing their part to get the project started.

This behavior is frustrating and infuriating to everyone, but the anxious-preoccupied are especially likely to protest by losing control of their own emotions and demanding attention through verbal or physical abuse. Studies seem to show more domestic violence is *initiated* by an anxious-preoccupied partner, while the avoidant only responds with violence after direct attack which overwhelms their normal emotional control.

As quoted previously:

> We also suspect that avoidant individuals display aggression indirectly, even if they are not prone to violence. They are likely to engage in "passive aggression," which includes expressions of indifference, disrespect, and contempt, and to use violence as a means of distancing themselves from a partner who will not leave them alone. These reactions, which fit comfortably with attachment-system deactivation, can easily be perceived by a partner as psychologically abusive, which might cause the partner to react aggressively. Thus, even if not directly aggressive themselves, avoidant partners may be involved in

mutually violent and abusive acts within a couple.[75]

It's important to remember that the avoidant is behaving reasonably under what they see as great provocation—they're doing their part, these demands for more are so irritating, why bother to respond to the endless prattle of the needy? Breaking this cycle will require them to step out of their pattern and recognize how they contribute to dysfunctional communication by not responding honestly and supportively in the first place and building up resentment in their partner. Showing them how passive-aggressive behavior aggravates their relationship difficulties is a start in turning them around.

Part Four

Happiness With an Avoidant

Chapter 25

Getting to Acceptance

Every relationship involves two people. Happiness and good communications between partners requires both to learn the steps of the dance—and if you are already deeply invested in your avoidant partner and have a shared history and family life to lose, it is usually not just the avoidant who needs to change to improve your lives together.

If you are reading this book, you already have some motivation for change. Getting your avoidant spouse or partner to read this book or enter counselling with you would be useful, but there are things you can do on your own to improve your relationship and make yourself and your avoidant happier.

First, you can commit to changing your own communication styles to be less irritating to the avoidant's dislike of dependence. If your partner is only half there for you when you request assistance, accept that they are never going to be as supportive as you might like and lower the volume and insistence of your own requests. Since your partner doesn't want to be as close as you like, you can accept it and cope by finding other support (from family and friends) or just stew in your own unhappy juices until something explodes. Continually telling yourself you deserve better and if you just try harder your avoidant will respond is a surefire way to drive them into more hidden anger and passive-aggressive withdrawal.

Second, you can develop outside friends and work interests that at least give you some of the satisfaction and support that you may be missing at home. If your work life is stressful and unfulfilling, having little support in your own home will make things worse. If you can't change your homelife much, you can often change things in the other spheres you spend time in (work, clubs, church, extended family) to increase your happiness.

Third, try to consider the good things about your partner. This might be a sense of humor, accomplishments in work or home projects, or occasional flashes of affection and gratitude (if you think back, there may have been some.) Are there things about your partner you would actually miss? Does imagining your avoidant partner's sudden death (in an accident, perhaps) remind you of your feelings for them, and make you wonder what you would do without their support with children and daily life? If you can't think of anything you'd miss, then you should probably not be continuing to stick with it.

I'll review some other topics in this section, then get into improving couples communication. Even doing your part in reducing your requests in frequency and insistence may help relieve some of the stresses in your relationship; and if not, you will have at least done what you could to try to make your avoidant more comfortable. If you cannot improve your relationship and your avoidant will not try to improve their behavior, you will then have to consider giving up and going it alone to look for someone more suitable; but don't give up until you've tried everything. No one benefits in a breakup, especially if you have younger children.

Chapter 26

Mark Manson's Advice

Internet philosopher Mark Manson is also a bit rough on the "fairy tale" conception of romance and relationships. The following is a riff on his post on healthy relationship habits:

> In his research of thousands of happily married couples, some of whom who have been married for 40+ years, he found time and again that most successful couples have persistent unresolved issues, unresolved issues that they've sometimes been fighting about for decades. Meanwhile many of the unsuccessful couples insisted on resolving fucking everything because they believed that there should be a void of disagreement between them. Pretty soon there was a void of a relationship too.[76]

I would say "disagreeing" rather than fighting. Constant fighting over anything is relationship-eroding. What he is getting at is that you can agree to disagree about something, discuss it from time to time, and not let negative feelings about it endanger your much more important relationship. Couples who fight over unimportant things because for one or both of them creating perfection is more important than the value of their partner as they are, warts and all, are headed for trouble. You can both be controlling perfectionists and still treasure each other's differences so long as you *mostly* agree on the ground rules of your home and heart. Over time these differences can become another source of playful banter and perspective. Picking at differences and showing hostility and contempt toward your partner for loading the dishwasher wrong or forgetting to put the toothpaste cap on is a sign of a relationship that won't last.

> It's important to make something more important in your
> relationship than merely making each other feel good all of the
> time. The feel good stuff happens when you get the other stuff
> right. The sunsets and puppies, they happen when you get the
> more important stuff right: values, needs and trust.

> If I feel smothered and need more time alone, I need to be
> capable of saying that without blaming her and she needs to be
> capable of hearing it without blaming me, despite the
> unpleasant feelings it may cause. If she feels that I'm cold and
> unresponsive to her, she needs to be capable of saying it
> without blaming me and I need to be capable of hearing it
> without blaming her, despite the unpleasant feelings it may
> generate.

> These conversations are paramount to maintaining a healthy
> relationship that meets both people's needs. With out them, we
> get lost and lose track of one another."

Supporting one another in the real world requires sympathetic
honesty—tactful tough love, not constant ego support by always
saying the thing you know will make your partner feel best.
Sometimes feeling good is not the path to success for your partner or
yourself—the truth about what you need and how you feel must be
told, even if you have a duty to speak it tactfully and kindly.
Otherwise the shared worldview of the couple won't be realistic,
leading to disappointment and distrust.

> Our cultural scripts for romance includes this sort of mental
> tyranny, where any mildly emotional or sexual thought not
> involving your partner amounts to high treason. Being in love
> is like a cult where you're supposed to prefer drinking Kool Aid
> laced with cyanide to letting your thoughts wander to whether

other religions may be true too.

As much as we'd like to believe that we only have eyes for our partner, biology says otherwise. Once we get past the honeymoon phase of starry eyes and oxytocin, the novelty of our partner wears off a bit. And unfortunately, human sexuality is partially wired around novelty. I get emails all the time from people in happy marriages/relationships who get blindsided by finding someone else attractive and they feel like horrible, horrible people because of it. Not only are we capable of finding multiple people attractive and interesting at the same time, but it's a biological inevitability.

What isn't an inevitability are our choices to act on it or not. Most of us, most of the time, choose to not act on those thoughts. And like waves, they pass through us and leave us with our partner very much the same way how they found us.

This triggers a lot of guilt in some people and a lot of irrational jealousy in others. Our cultural scripts tell us that once we're in love, that's supposed to be it, end of story. And if someone flirts with us and we enjoy it, or if we catch ourselves having an occasional errant sexy-time fantasy, there must be something wrong with us or our relationship.

But that's simply not the case. In fact, it's healthier to allow oneself to experience these feelings and then let them go.[78]

This is a key point. Our evolutionary heritage has left us with multiple levels of motivation: rational/logical, emotional, and instinctive. One level (instinctive) is able to throw biochemical switches to enable urges that are intended to drive us to act in ways that might have, in some past environment, been of advantage to ourselves and our children. But as we mature through adolescence, we gain more and more rational control over these feelings—knowing the consequences will be bad, we stop ourselves from acting on so-called base urges, and avoid pawing the attractive co-worker or accepting the offer of sex from an attractive other which will likely damage your life. But those motivations are not themselves wrong—they are part of you! Feeling attraction and enjoying occasional flirting are not something to feel guilty about. Pretending you never feel them is dishonest and sets you up to fail by falling for them when you think you won't get caught—you're being dishonest with yourself, so it becomes easier to be dishonest with your partner.

> People who suppress these urges are the ones who are likely to eventually succumb to them and give in and suddenly find themselves screwing the secretary in the broom closet and having no idea how they got there and come to deeply regret it about twenty-two seconds afterward. People who suppress these urges are the ones who are likely to project them onto their partner and becoming blindingly jealous, attempting to control their partner's every thought and whim, corralling all of their partner's attention and affection onto themselves. People who suppress these urges are the ones who are likely to wake up one day disgruntled and frustrated with no conscious understanding of why, wondering where all of the days went and remember how in love we used to be?[79]

It's inevitable that you, as an attractive member of an attractive couple, will get attention and offers from others, and encounter people who you develop some limerence toward. The wise choice is to view this feeling as proof that you are alive and functioning as a human being, enjoy the feeling, and only act on it as you can without damaging people you love.

It's very important to recognize the power of limerence and sexual attraction to get our attention when we're in along-term relationship. Foolish people listen to the Siren call of hormones and destroy good marriages that have a history and security to pursue a temporary obsession; this mistake can destroy lives and damage your children. Cultivate the mental detachment to enjoy and be entertained by these hormonal storms without losing your grip on reality; recognize it is no more likely to last than a weekend bender, and take care to reassure your partner that you are committed to them despite this distraction, since there's no way you can hide such feelings from someone really close to you. Bring your partner in on this temporary insanity and ask for their forbearance. Because you are in this together. And if your partner is in the grip of Fairy Tale thinking, you have to snap them out of it.

Chapter 27

Stable is Boring?

As to why you may have ended up with your avoidant partner: evolution may have left you with a preference for apparently desirable sexual partners over others who would provide a stable home life.

Attachment studies and *Psychology Today* agree: women especially have a problem they need to recognize. The kind of intensely activating, sexy and dominant partner they may crave is the least likely to be a good long-term mate. A *Psychology Today* column by Jeremy Nicholson has some good bits:

> Dating and relationships have always been hard. In this day and age, however, they can sometimes seem impossible. Particularly, women I speak to say that they can't find a good man. They lament over the guys that they say are stuck in childhood, not taking responsibility for their lives. They complain about the men they call "nice guy, push-over" types, who don't stir passionate feelings. They also have difficulty with men they label attractive "jerks", who disrespect them, ignore their needs, and break hearts.[80]

This states the general problem: for anxious-preoccupied women (but for others as well), the "nice," sensitive, thoughtful guys don't wake them up even though they might be the wisest choice for partnering up with. Meanwhile, the rough, aggressive, dominating sorts giving off testosterone and sexual fitness get their attention, but can't be relied on and may well end up being abusive. A Secure person will tend to react against the thoughtless and self-centered and so avoid the harm these "bad boys" do, but for the insecure this drama-filled interaction—with intermittent reinforcement, sexual excitement, and extra-strong hormones—is a lure that's hard to stay away from even when they know it's not a good choice.

Socially, today's woman is encouraged, empowered (and perhaps expected) to do it all. This, in itself, often causes extreme stress for the "super woman" and "super mom." Social norms tell her she is expected to succeed in work, run her home, raise the perfect children, and be attractive and chipper too. It is a tall order. It is also an order that requires women to be intelligent, motivated, powerful, and in control.

Given those social instructions, women are motivated to "choose" men for how well they mesh with their life plan, goals, and ideals. Essentially then, some women choose to "attach" to men who are cooperative, agreeable, supportive, and often take their lead in areas the woman finds important. From a cultural standpoint, men who are categorized as "disagreeable," "opinionated," or expect women to "acquiesce" may be considered unappealing as long-term partners.

Unfortunately, however, many of those "culturally undesirable" male traits are similar and overlapping with the traits that are biologically "attractive." Although not always true, often the man who is intelligent, high status, and ambitious will be unlikely to take a back seat, follow, and submit in a romantic relationship. Generally speaking, men who have "leadership characteristics" may want to lead in many situations.

With those two "feelings" juxtaposed, women often find themselves unfulfilled in love. Many that I talk to seem to hover between what they call "nice guys" and "jerks" in their dating life. They become attracted to "jerks" for their status, ambition, and dominance—only to be hurt when those men don't live up to the cooperative and considerate cultural standard for an attachment partner. Women then may gravitate towards a culturally prescribed "nice guy," only to find that they become bored, their libido wanes, and their eyes wander back to "jerks." Either way, they find the relationships largely frustrating and unsatisfying.[81]

The new customs have delayed marriage, leaving an expected period (college years until 30 or so) of experimentation and "finding yourself." There is concern about the "sexual carousel" (or more rudely, the "cock carousel"), of *Sex and the City*-style promiscuity or rapid serial monogamy. Sexually exciting partners are tried and found wanting over and over, until finally the young person is no longer young and realizes the most obviously exciting are not the partners who will stick by you no matter what. And by that time, most the best partners have already bonded and are unavailable, so what's left is more avoidant, more used up, and more set in their ways.

The article goes on to suggest some strategies (for women, but it's valid for everyone):

1) Learning to Love Leading—one strategy adopted by some women is to learn to love being the leader of a "nice guy". Think empowered business woman, cougar, or even dominatrix. All of these women relish being in charge, empowered, and having their desires fulfilled. Getting what you want can be pretty attractive after all. This dominant approach may have a downside in resentment and rebellion however. So, be considerate (and persuasive)....

2) Following Wisely—other women choose to be cautious in love, looking for the "right" guy to be with, and enjoying their attraction to strong, male leadership. This is more of the compatibility, eHarmony approach. These women evaluate and "test" men to find the right guy, a guy who will lead with their

hopes, dreams, and goals in mind. They know that, if you're not driving, it is wise to pick the driver carefully. Thus, they find a man with strong, attractive attributes to swoon over, who will not end up treating them like a "jerk...."

3) Mixed-Mating—yet other women join the "best of both worlds" club. Here, think polyamory, open relationships, or a hot boyfriend on the side. Evolutionary psychology indicates that women sometimes use this strategy to seek the most stable and supportive partnership from one man, and the best genes for children from another. When women can't find it all in one guy, some choose to mix-and-match....

4) Negotiation, Sharing, and Balance—finally, some women choose to negotiate and share leadership roles with their partner. They divide life tasks and duties into different areas, with each being the "boss" of different things. Perhaps she leads with the finances, and he takes charge of the kids (or vice versa). That way, everyone has a bit of leadership, responsibility, agreeableness...and therefore attraction and attachment too.

This is too simple—animal dominance and submission is not the best model for human partnerships or marriage. We are far more sophisticated as a species, and good marriages typically have a division of labor as in choice 4, so that one partner tends to handle some kinds of tasks while the other partner does others; this specialization makes the marriage stronger because tasks are handled by the most competent member at that type of task. In a good marriage of equals, both partners leave decisionmaking in some spheres to the other, and even the most aggressive and dominant in, say, external business affairs is not threatened by ceding control of, say, entertaining to the other; and nothing says this has to be conventional. Most of us know a couple where the husband is the great cook and the wife handles all the investments. This happens naturally for the most part, without any conscious negotiation—it's not bargaining for dominance.

The "best of both worlds" club ("polyamory, open relationships, or a hot boyfriend on the side") is controversial. One of modern men's resentments is that women will accept the support of a good man, then pursue cheating with sexually exciting bad boys; of course stereotypically this was always something "bad boys" did, having a respectable "madonna" wife at home while chasing "whore" skirt on the side (see *Mad Men* for examples of how it used to be for upper-class men!) It goes against the grain of both societal expectations and evolutionary psychology for males to tolerate being used to support children of less responsible men, so open marriages with honest pursuit of outside sexual partners are likely to remain a minority choice for couples able to have children. But the excitement of cheating will always tempt those who crave more stimulation, and so one of our primary sources of fictional and real-life drama will continue.

Chapter 28

Parental Preferences in Partners

This chapter, like the last, discusses why you might have been attracted to your unsupportive avoidant partner even though your parents (and your rational side) may have had doubts.

From "Evolution and Bad Boyfriends," a *New York Times* piece on the struggle between parents and (most commonly) daughters over partner choice and how it may have evolved:

> Whenever a pattern of human behavior is widespread, there is reason to suspect that it might have something to do with our evolutionary history. (Think of the fear of snakes, or the incest taboo.) You think your daughter's boyfriend isn't good enough? It may be evolution's fault.[82]

Now I generally argue against easy "ev psych" (Evolutionary Psychology) answers for questions of human behavior. But when you look at the commonalities across cultures around the world, you do find evidence of an ev-psych background that sets the stage for the much more complex cultural norms that have evolved. And many traditional cultures do have parents playing a significant or even primary role in mate selection for their offspring; arranged marriages and dowries were commonly used to assure a good match for a daughter, who would leave her parents' household to join her new husband's.

> When thinking about mate choice, the natural starting point is the theory of sexual selection. This theory, which focuses not

on the struggle for existence but on the competition to attract sexual partners, has been hugely successful in explaining the diverse courtship behaviors and mating patterns in the animal kingdom, from the peacock's flamboyant tail to the chirping calls of male crickets.

Modern mathematical versions of this theory show how female mating preferences and male characteristics will evolve together. But when you try to apply the theory to humans, you hit a snag. In humans, there is an extra preference involved— that of the parents.

At first sight, it might seem surprising that parents and their children should evolve to have any conflict at all. After all, they share many of the same genes, and both have an evolutionary interest in having those genes persist through the generations. Shouldn't the preferences of parents and their children be perfectly aligned?

Well, no—not completely. Parents each pass on half of their genes to each of their children, so from a genetic point of view, all children are equally valuable to them. It is in parents' evolutionary interests to distribute their resources—money, support, etc.—in such a way that leads to as many surviving grandchildren as possible, regardless of which of their children provide them.

Children, by contrast, have a stronger genetic interest in their own reproduction than in that of their siblings, so each child should try to secure more than his or her fair share of parental resources. It is this conflict over parental resources that can lead to a conflict over mate choice.

In our study, we built a computer model to simulate the evolutionary process. We generated a large virtual population of males and females, the males all differing genetically in their ability to invest resources in raising children. The females had a genetically determined preference for this male quality, which meant that females with a strong preference were more likely to end up with a male who invested more.

The males and females that paired up in our model then mated and produced offspring, who inherited (with a small chance of mutation) the investing qualities and mating preferences of their parents. We ran our model over thousands of generations, observing which genetic traits thrived and which didn't.[83]

This is a *genetic algorithm,* the kind of computer simulation I used to write to discover behavioral tendencies among populations of stock traders. Like all simulations, it can only be suggestive because good results depend on duplicating the important features of both the simulated people and their environment; but it can reveal the underlying reason why certain traits and behaviors are preserved and strengthened over time.

...We added some new ingredients. First, we allowed a female's parents to interfere with her choice of a male. Second, we allowed parents to distribute their resources among their children.

We found that over time, parents in our model evolved to invest more resources in daughters who chose mates with few resources. This unequal investment was in the parents' best interests, because a daughter with an unsupportive partner would profit more from extra help than her more fortunate sisters (the principle of diminishing returns on investment). By helping their needier daughters, parents maximized their total number of surviving grandchildren.

But this unequal investment created an incentive for daughters to "exploit" their parents' generosity by choosing a partner who was less supportive. A daughter who was less picky than her sisters would accept a less helpful partner, but since her parents picked up the slack she ended up with a similar amount of support, while sparing herself the costs of holding out for the perfect man.

As a result, the choosiness of females gradually declined over evolutionary time. To counterbalance this, the parental preference for caring sons-in-law increased. Hence the conflict.[84]

It is only in the modern era that it became safe in the West for daughters to strike out on their own and put off marriage while gaining independence; parental control over mate selection is now much weaker than in traditional societies. And yet the evolved preferences for "bad boys" and the expectation that parents would come to a daughter's assistance if resources were short as a result of the bad husband's unreliability continued. Now that it is a woman's choice, the chances have increased that young women will choose unwisely, because whatever part of her preferences are innate was evolved when her parents were a key safeguard in keeping her from making bad choices.

Chapter 29

Soulmates or Fellow Travelers?

Expecting a perfect marriage or partnership ("soulmates") implies your partner is perfect. Since no one is perfect, such expectations are doomed to disappoint, and some research out of U Toronto reports that couples who think of their marriage or partnership as a journey are happier with their relationships and more resistant to negative thoughts:

> Psychologists observe that people talk and think about love in apparently limitless ways but underlying such diversity are some common themes that frame how we think about relationships. For example, one popular frame considers love as perfect unity ("made for each other," "she's my other half"); in another frame, love is a journey ("look how far we've come," "we've been through all these things together"). These two ways of thinking about relationships are particularly interesting because, according to study authors social psychologists Spike W. S. Lee of the University of Toronto's Rotman School of Management and Norbert Schwarz of the University of Southern California, they have the power to highlight or downplay the damaging effect of conflicts on relationship evaluation. Here's why. If two people were really made in heaven for each other, why should they have any conflicts?

> "Our findings corroborate prior research showing that people who implicitly think of relationships as perfect unity between soulmates have worse relationships than people who implicitly think of relationships as a journey of growing and working

things out," says Prof. Lee. "Apparently, different ways of talking and thinking about love relationship lead to different ways of evaluating it."

In one experiment, Profs. Lee and Schwarz had people in long-term relationships complete a knowledge quiz that included expressions related to either unity or journey, then recall either conflicts or celebrations with their romantic partner, and finally evaluate their relationship. As predicted, recalling conflicts leads people to feel less satisfied with their relationship—but only with the unity frame in mind, not with the journey frame in mind. Recalling celebrations makes people satisfied with their relationship regardless of how they think about it.

In a two follow-up experiments, the study authors invoked the unity vs. journey frame in even subtler, more incidental ways. For example, people were asked to identify pairs of geometric shapes to form a full circle (activating unity) or draw a line that gets from point A to point B through a maze (activating journey). Such non-linguistic, merely pictorial cues were sufficient to change the way people evaluated relationships. Again, conflicts hurt relationship satisfaction with the unity frame in mind, not with the journey frame in mind.

Next time you and your partner have a conflict, as Profs. Lee and Schwarz would advise, think what you said at the altar, "I, _____, take you, _____, to be my husband/wife, to have and to hold from this day forward, for better, for worse, for richer, for poorer, in sickness or in health, to love and to cherish; from this day forward 'till death do us part." It's a journey. You'll feel better now, and you'll do better down the road.[85]

How much of your unhappiness with your avoidant is due to your expectations of finding a soulmate with whom you can have perfect communication and intimacy? If you were expecting that, probably any normal human being, even a secure type with good communications skills and empathy, is going to be disappointing some of the time. Whereas if you can empathize with your dismissive partner and see the world through their eyes (even when they can't do the same for you), you may find understanding that their path as also a difficult one may help you handle the emotional stress of their relatively poor responsiveness. If the two of you aren't perfectly suited to each other, perhaps you are still suitable traveling companions.

Chapter 30

The Destructive Fairy Tale Model

In *Bad Boyfriends,* I discussed the problems of the "Fairy Tale model." This fantasy of a perfect relationship satisfying your every need is crippling for both men and women; yet one reviewer took me to task for supposed misogyny when I pointed out that little girls brought up to think of themselves as fairy tale princesses entitled to effortless happiness were likely to find the real world difficult and disappointing. But it is equally disappointing for young men to discover that their courage and willingness to rescue a fair damsel in distress does not usually get them the girl, unlike in the stories; young women looking for Prince Charming tend to discount socially awkward but courageous young men unless they are at the top of the local social ladder.

When the arranged-marriage, marriage-for-property-and-dynasty system went out of style, marriages became a choose-for-yourself project, with a much larger pool of candidates to choose from. While this freed many to find more compatible partners, it also cast the losers into a game of musical relationship chairs where most of the remaining candidates were problematic; 50% of the population have insecure attachment types, and freedom of choice meant those insecure people were more often thrown in together into dysfunctional marriages. No longer feeling obligated to make a marriage work, and finding a year or two in that their partner is either too controlling and clingy or too cold and avoidant the sniping and the negative communication games begin. You could call this another facet of assortative mating, where the best partners find each other and leave the worst to deal with each other.

There's also a selection effect: we notice the marriages where people fight or snipe at each other. The half of marriages that do well do so quietly, and it's easy to assume married people treat each other badly behind the scenes when nearly everyone tries to maintain status and self-image by presenting a falsely positive view to outsiders. Those whose marriages are happy tend to quietly enjoy themselves and get on with their lives, while the unhappy participants in bad marriages are more likely to let everyone know just how awful their partner is, after presenting a glowing but false picture at first.

There is a real world, and a couple has to join together and face reality as partners to be successful both with each other and in surviving and thriving in a sometimes harsh environment. A real partnership grows stronger with adversity overcome by mutual effort; if one or both partners think life should be easy because they are goodlooking, or great at sports, or Daddy's Little Girl, the normal setbacks of life will have them blaming their partner and running for the exit. Happiness —or great sex or a perfect house—is not the immediate goal of a successful relationship; the goal is a bond that strengthens both of you and helps you be more the person you want to be. Happiness in marriage, when it happens, is a byproduct of love and loyalty and accomplishments together over time.

Belief in the Fairy Tale Model is crippling, often leaving believers battered, poorer, and alone in middle age—ask many of the bewildered divorced fathers, who are *eight times* more likely to commit suicide than divorced women.[86] And the divorcées, having moved on to what they expected would be sexier, more attentive men? Having thrown away their shared history and often damaged their children by depriving them of a father's guidance, their lives are not improved. What they wanted was an illusion.

An article in *Psychology Today* blogs gets at what's happening to many marriages today as a result of the Fairy Tale model, combined with social support for divorce and "you can have it all" attitudes. The author-therapist, Randi Gunther, Ph.D., sees more and more breakups where the husbands have been close to the ideals the young wives say they want—but the wives are unsatisfied anyway:

> The women I have treated who have left their husbands for more "masculine" men believed that their new relationships would be able to both excite and nurture them. Sadly, that has not always happened. The veritable saint with balls is as elusive as ever.

> When things haven't worked out as they thought they would, several of the women I am now working with are re-thinking their decisions, wondering if they left too soon, or for the wrong reasons. They want to reconcile with the men they have left behind. Their husbands are torn between the understandable desire to reject them and still wanting them back. Ironically, because these have nurtured the feminine side of their natures, they are also able to forgive in a way few men have been able to do in the past. But because they have no interest in returning to the "bad boy" mentality their competitors brandished, they are faced with a challenge most men have never had to confront. How do they hold on to their vulnerability and capacity to nurture, and blend it with the strength and power required of a self-respecting leader of men?[87]

These women think they want a good partner and helpmate, but found themselves missing the thrill of the bad boys that excite their attachment systems. It's a shame they disrupted what they acknowledge were good marriages wanting something more that generally doesn't exist in real life.

Chapter 31

Subconscious Attitudes Signal Outcomes

Another study reminds us how critical reasonable expectations are to happiness. If you are inclined to have positive attitudes and respect for your partner as you begin your marriage, you are more likely to have a happy and successful marriage. Seems obvious, but apparently many people enter into marriage with partners they have negative views of. How can this be? Because a surprising number of people get married for convenience, to meet societal expectations, because they think they might as well....

Subconscious positive attitudes predict marriage success, and conversely, negativity predicts turmoil and failure. In attachment type terms, both avoidant types (Dismissive- and Fearful-Avoidant) have a negative view of attached others in general, while Secure and Anxious-Preoccupied types are positive about others.

The Wall Street Journal, in the story "New Ways to Predict Which Marriages Will Succeed," reports on an experiment which measures newlywed's subconscious attitudes about their partners and found those with negative subconscious attitudes experienced a faster decline in marital satisfaction over time:

> First off, they found that ratings of marital satisfaction declined over time, something reported previously. They also learned that the [written test] answers from newlyweds predicted nothing about marital satisfaction four years later.

> But the scientists also measured something else in those

newlyweds, using an "associative priming task." This involves briefly flashing a series of words like "wonderful" or "odious" on a screen; subjects have to quickly press one of two buttons, depending on whether the word has positive or negative connotations. Now comes the subconscious manipulation.

Just before each word, the researchers flashed up a picture of a random face for an instant—300 milliseconds—too fast for people to be consciously certain about what they saw but enough time for our subconscious, emotional brain circuitry to be certain. If the face evokes positive feelings, the brain immediately takes on something akin to a positive mind-set; if the word flashed up an instant later is a positive one, the brain quickly detects it as such. But if the word is negative, there is an instant of subconscious dissonance—"I was feeling great, but now I have to think about that word that means 'inconsiderate jerk who doesn't replace the toilet paper.'" And it takes a few milliseconds longer to hit the "negative" key. Conversely, display faces with negative connotations, and there is that dissonance-induced minuscule delay in identifying positive terms.

So in the study, the rapid-fire sequence of faces/words included a picture of one's new spouse, revealing automatic feelings about the person's beloved. That led to the key finding: The more subconscious negativity in a newlywed, the larger the decline in marital satisfaction four years later.

Did subjects understand what the priming task was about? No, and people's automatic responses were unrelated to their answers on the questionnaire. Was that discrepancy due to an unwillingness to answer honestly, or were people unaware of their automatic attitudes? It is impossible to tell. Did people with the most positive automatic feelings about their spouses subsequently develop fewer problems in their marriages, or were they less sensitive to the usual number of problems? Subtle data analysis suggested the latter.

What does this study tell us, beyond suggesting that lovebirds should probably take this nifty computerized test before marrying? It reminds us, like much we learn about the brain and behavior, that we are subject to endless, internal biological forces of which we are unaware.[88]

It's a shame this or a similar test revealing subconscious attitudes isn't used to screen out bad matches before years of turmoil and tragic family breakups. I was discussing this with a women I know who is the event planner for a local wedding venue; she claims you could just ask her and she would be right 90% of the time in predicting which couples won't last simply based on her observations of how they treated each other during the wedding planning, and I suspect she is right.

Part Five

Changing Communication Styles

Chapter 32

Couples Therapy

In couples therapy or marriage counselling, the relationship itself is the focus of therapy. This will often mean some suggestions for individual therapy for the members of the family, but it is rarely the primary focus since marriage counselling tries to change how spouses treat each other and their children, and deep attachment issues of each spouse are beyond the time and resources available—couples normally start counselling far too late, when divorce is being talked about.

Marriage counsellors vary widely in quality and methods (as is true of all counsellors and therapists.) Simply being licensed by a government is no guarantee they have any wisdom or ability to help correct any but the most superficial problems in a relationship. They tend to avoid taking sides—even when the dysfunction is largely due to one spouse's issues—and in the modern era will often be too quick to advise divorce when one partner is avoidant, especially when that partner is often apparently cruel or uncaring. Look for a couples therapist who will take the time to sort out your attachment issues and work with both of you to improve levels of empathy and effective communication.

In the chapter "Best Practices for Couples," the work of the Gottman Institute is cited as the best guidance for couples whose communications styles are making their relationships unhappy. Couples therapists who use Gottman materials are more likely to understand the problems of your relationship and have effective ideas for improving communication. These are based on the basic patterns discussed in the chapter Touch and Response, and show how troubled relationships can be improved by simply avoiding the unsatisfactory patterns through empathy and mindful change of behavior.

Dr. John Gottman's *The Seven Principles for Making Marriage Work* is a highly-recommended book treatment of some of their principles—a good read for both of you. The Gottman Institute web site also has video courses and in-person workshops if you are interested. The best treatment of their ideas online is an excellent article by Emily Esfahani Smith in *The Atlantic*. After studying how newlywed couples relate, they identified relationship "masters" and "disasters" and how each type functioned:

> Gottman wanted to know more about how the masters created that culture of love and intimacy, and how the disasters squashed it. In a follow-up study in 1990, he designed a lab on the University of Washington campus to look like a beautiful bed and breakfast retreat. He invited 130 newlywed couples to spend the day at this retreat and watched them as they did what couples normally do on vacation: cook, clean, listen to music, eat, chat, and hang out. And Gottman made a critical discovery in this study—one that gets at the heart of why some relationships thrive while others languish.

> Throughout the day, partners would make requests for connection, what Gottman calls "bids." For example, say that the husband is a bird enthusiast and notices a goldfinch fly across the yard. He might say to his wife, "Look at that beautiful bird outside!" He's not just commenting on the bird here: he's requesting a response from his wife—a sign of interest or support—hoping they'll connect, however momentarily, over the bird.

> The wife now has a choice. She can respond by either "turning

toward" or "turning away" from her husband, as Gottman puts it. Though the bird-bid might seem minor and silly, it can actually reveal a lot about the health of the relationship. The husband thought the bird was important enough to bring it up in conversation and the question is whether his wife recognizes and respects that.

> People who turned toward their partners in the study responded by engaging the bidder, showing interest and support in the bid. Those who didn't—those who turned away —would not respond or respond minimally and continue doing whatever they were doing, like watching TV or reading the paper. Sometimes they would respond with overt hostility, saying something like, "Stop interrupting me, I'm reading."[89]

Of course the latter is dismissive behavior, corresponding to the distancing communications styles. Dr. Gottman identified it as the best predictor of relationship unhappiness and dissolution:

> These bidding interactions had profound effects on marital well-being. Couples who had divorced after a six-year follow up had "turn-toward bids" 33 percent of the time. Only three in ten of their bids for emotional connection were met with intimacy. The couples who were still together after six years had "turn-toward bids" 87 percent of the time. Nine times out of ten, they were meeting their partner's emotional needs.[90]

Most of the Gottman Institute's methods for improving marriages hinge on this insight. Knowing your spouse well, being able to empathize and predict what they are probably feeling and thinking, and making your requests for attention in light of that understanding —and responding to them positively as much as possible—is key to effective and satisfying communication. Happiness comes from those moments of effective support, and the confidence (based on thousands of small but positive interactions) that your spouse will be there for you in a real crisis.

> "There's a habit of mind that the masters have," Gottman explained in an interview, "which is this: they are scanning social environment for things they can appreciate and say thank you for. They are building this culture of respect and appreciation very purposefully. Disasters are scanning the social environment for partners' mistakes."

> "It's not just scanning environment," chimed in Julie Gottman. "It's scanning the partner for what the partner is doing right or scanning him for what he's doing wrong and criticizing versus respecting him and expressing appreciation."

Contempt, they have found, is the number one factor that tears couples apart. People who are focused on criticizing their partners miss a whopping 50 percent of positive things their partners are doing and they see negativity when it's not there. People who give their partner the cold shoulder—deliberately ignoring the partner or responding minimally—damage the relationship by making their partner feel worthless and invisible, as if they're not there, not valued. And people who treat their partners with contempt and criticize them not only kill the love in the relationship, but they also kill their partner's ability to fight off viruses and cancers. Being mean is the death knell of relationships.

Kindness, on the other hand, glues couples together. Research independent from theirs has shown that kindness (along with emotional stability) is the most important predictor of satisfaction and stability in a marriage. Kindness makes each partner feel cared for, understood, and validated—feel loved. "My bounty is as boundless as the sea," says Shakespeare's Juliet. "My love as deep; the more I give to thee, / The more I have, for both are infinite." That's how kindness works too: there's a great deal of evidence showing the more someone receives or witnesses kindness, the more they will be kind themselves, which leads to upward spirals of love and generosity in a relationship.[91]

An Avoidant who wants to improve communication can practice to give more positive responses even when their impulse is to deny response or respond negatively; and correspondingly, if their partner is an Anxious-Preoccupied type, the partner can work on curbing the impulse to request attention and reassurance when not really necessary, or when the Avoidant is busy or irritated. In both cases, one needs to understand how it feels to be the other partner, and tune your request or response to their needs as well as your own. Cultivate the habit of considering your partner's state before responding carelessly or asking for reassurance, and the relationship is much more likely to feel satisfying and truly supportive.

> There are two ways to think about kindness. You can think about it as a fixed trait: either you have it or you don't. Or you could think of kindness as a muscle. In some people, that muscle is naturally stronger than in others, but it can grow stronger in everyone with exercise. Masters tend to think about kindness as a muscle. They know that they have to exercise it to keep it in shape. They know, in other words, that a good relationship requires sustained hard work.

> "If your partner expresses a need," explained Julie Gottman, "and you are tired, stressed, or distracted, then the generous spirit comes in when a partner makes a bid, and you still turn toward your partner."

In that moment, the easy response may be to turn away from your partner and focus on your iPad or your book or the television, to mumble "Uh huh" and move on with your life, but neglecting small moments of emotional connection will slowly wear away at your relationship. Neglect creates distance between partners and breeds resentment in the one who is being ignored.[92]

The trouble with all of this healthy advice is the difficulty the avoidant partner has in seeing any of it as important enough to work on. Their blockade of positive attachment feelings means it is hard to motivate them to change anything much, and they view others as the primary source of relationship problems. To overcome this, it is necessary to draw them into a rational discussion of their (and your!) attachment issues and communications patterns; if you get them as far as reading this book, you will have started a process that may eventually lead them to enough insight to make a real effort to change.

I'll close with the "Gottman Method for Healthy Relationships:"

1. Build Love Maps: How well do you know your partner's inner psychological world, his or her history, worries, stresses, joys, and hopes?

2. Share Fondness and Admiration: The antidote for contempt, this level focuses on the amount of affection and respect within a relationship. (To strengthen fondness and admiration, express appreciation and respect.)

3. Turn Towards: State your needs, be aware of bids for connection and respond to (turn towards) them. The small moments of everyday life are actually the building blocks of relationship.

4. The Positive Perspective: The presence of a positive approach to problem-solving and the success of repair attempts.

5. Manage Conflict: We say "manage" conflict rather than "resolve" conflict, because relationship conflict is natural and

has functional, positive aspects. Understand that there is a critical difference in handling perpetual problems and solvable problems.

6. Make Life Dreams Come True: Create an atmosphere that encourages each person to talk honestly about his or her hopes, values, convictions and aspirations.

7. Create Shared Meaning: Understand important visions, narratives, myths, and metaphors about your relationship.

8. Trust: this is the state that occurs when a person knows that his or her partner acts and thinks to maximize that person's best interests and benefits, not just the partner's own interests and benefits. In other words, this means, "my partner has my back and is there for me."

9. Commitment: This means believing (and acting on the belief) that your relationship with this person is completely your lifelong journey, for better or for worse (meaning that if it gets worse you will both work to improve it). It implies cherishing your partner's positive qualities and nurturing gratitude by comparing the partner favorably with real or imagined others, rather than trashing the partner by magnifying negative qualities, and nurturing resentment by comparing unfavorably with real or imagined others.[93]

Chapter 33

Individual Therapy

Attachment issues, especially those of the Dismissive- or Fearful-Avoidant, are deeply entrenched, and the Dismissive's blocked emotional memories and denial of needs for attachment make them especially tough subjects for therapy. Over a longer term, though, once they make a connection to a therapist who can reach through their walls, there is evidence they can overcome some of their issues:

> In contrast, Fonagy et al. (1996) found that although secure clients (assessed with the AAI) tended to function better than insecure clients at both admission into and discharge from individual or group psychoanalytic therapy (lasting more than 9 months), avoidant clients exhibited the greatest amount of improvement over the course of treatment. According to B. Meyer and Pilkonis (2001), this finding may be attributable to the special benefits of long-term therapy for avoidant clients: "Those with dismissing attachment may require concentrated or targeted interventions, helping them overcome their characteristic detachment. Once they do connect emotionally with a therapist, however, improvement might be all the more dramatic" (p. 467).[94]

Even if you manage to get your avoidant partner to agree to long-term therapy, finding a therapist with a good understanding of attachment issues can be difficult. Quoting from *Bad Boyfriends:*

Group therapy, while valuable for getting feedback on the realism of your expectations and the actions you have taken to reach them, rarely is deep and focused enough to resolve attachment issues—the exception would be group therapy focused on one attachment type so that everyone's issues are similar, but that is hard to find.

In the United States and most other countries, expect to pay for individual therapy yourself. Under most medical insurance plans, an attachment issue is unlikely to be considered worthy of coverage; you can see a psychiatrist to be prescribed a psychoactive drug, or you can see a therapist (often chosen from a limited selection, with specialists in attachment unlikely to be among them) a few times before further authorization requiring a diagnosis is required. After that you will generally be on your own. And it's almost certainly true that you will find better therapists and more knowledgeable therapists if you pay their fee yourself; if your income is limited, ask the therapists you are considering if they will charge you a sliding scale fee, lower for long-term treatment on a limited income. Seeing a therapist your insurance will cover is a good way to start out, but if you find that experience unhelpful ask for referrals to more specialized therapists....

Sources of information on therapists and their specialties are hard to find. One online directory that has a critical mass of therapist listings for the US and Canada is Psychology Today's "Find a Therapist." But there are dozens of directories and many listings are unspecific about specialties; many therapists know very little about attachment. So seeking out a therapist who is familiar with the Dismissive- or Fearful-Avoidant is likely to involve searching, asking around, and calling to discuss the issues your partner has directly.

In Dr. Lewis' *A General Theory of Love*, he describes therapy in poetic language as a process where the therapist and the patient journey together, experiencing each other's feelings and letting the patient view his or her own interior thoughts and feelings as seen though the eyes of the therapist. The therapist serves as a secure anchor that can (metaphorically) pull the storm-tossed ship of the patient's emotional life toward a calmer shore. This only works, of course, if the patient is open to thinking about and describing his or her feelings, which is especially hard for the dismissive—the therapist may have to read between the lines and sharply question the patient's stories and rationalizations. It may take many sessions before the patient picks up the ability to dig through his or her own feelings with more insight to hold up the interesting discoveries to the light for the therapist to see.

> An attuned therapist feels the lure of a patient's limbic Attractors. He doesn't just hear about an emotional life—the two of them live it. The gravitational tug of this patient's emotional world draws him away from his own, just as it should. A determined therapist does not strive to have a good relationship with his patient— it can't be done. If a patient's emotional mind would support good relationships, he or she would be out having them. Instead a therapist loosens his grip on his own world and drifts, eyes open, into whatever relationship the patient has in mind—even a connection so dark that it touches the worst in him. He has no alternative. When he stays outside the other's world, he cannot affect it; when he steps within its range, he feels the force of alien Attractors. He takes up temporary residence in another's world not just to observe but to alter, and in the end, to overthrow. Through the intimacy a limbic exchange affords, therapy becomes the ultimate inside job.[95]

More extreme Dismissive-Avoidants may suffer from *alexithymia,* the inability to describe feelings in words:

> The most compelling theory of how consciousness arose has between-person communication (primitive language) giving rise to internal communication, so that what we see as a stream of consciousness is actually internal dialogue, talking to yourself. Noting this, you might say that an inability to name and talk about feelings cripples your ability to be consciously

aware of them. If one is very poor at doing this, one would tend to note feelings only as manifested in somatic symptoms like fast heart rate, discomfort, loss of energy, nervousness, etc.

This is why talking to someone about how you feel (or writing about it) is also training for being conscious of feelings internally. The more you talk about it to others, the more you can talk about it to yourself. Even for those not suffering from alexithymia, talking or writing about feelings can clarify understanding of them, which is one of the reasons talk therapy is effective.

Dr. Karen, in *Becoming Attached,* discusses this phenomenon of verbally describing a feeling to allow it to come under conscious control as its source is recognized:

Main's work supports an assumption on which much of psychoanalytic treatment is based: that being able to put feelings, especially unwanted feelings, into words makes them available for review and transformation.... To have this ability means, in effect, that your internal model is still a "working" model—open, flexible, able to assimilate new information. It means not only the ability to rethink the past but to recognize that people can be different and that their behavior doesn't always mean what we think it does. The criticism of a husband or wife, for example, may feel like an intentional assault on one's identity. If you are able to attend to the feeling and put it into words—"I feel worthless and debased, convinced he wants to get rid of me, and insanely anxious and needy"—then you are in a much better position than the person who reflexively acts out such feelings by becoming depressed and over-eating or becoming uncontrollably rageful.[96]

When therapy is successful, it can not only change dysfunctional patterns of attachment behavior, but also free the patient from other habits and assumptions picked up from parents and childhood experiences and carried through life as unquestioned givens:

> The first part of emotional healing is being limbically known—having someone with a keen ear catch your melodic essence. A child with emotionally hazy parents finds trying to know himself like wandering around a museum in the dark: almost anything could exist within its walls. He cannot ever be sure of what he senses. For adults, a precise seer's light can still split the night, illuminate treasures long thought lost, and dissolve many fearsome figures into shadows and dust. Those who succeed in revealing themselves to another find the dimness receding from their own visions of self. Like people awakening from a dream, they slough off the accumulated, ill-fitting trappings of unsuitable lives. Then the mutual fund manager may become a sculptor, or vice versa; some friendships lapse into dilapidated irrelevance as new ones deepen; the city dweller moves to the country, where he feels finally at home. As limbic clarity emerges, a life takes form.[97]

Chapter 34

Self-Directed Change

> Self-help books are like car repair manuals: you can read them
> all day, but doing so doesn't fix a thing. Working on a car
> means rolling up your sleeves and getting under the hood, and
> you have to be willing to get dirt on your hands and grease
> beneath your fingernails. Overhauling emotional knowledge is
> no spectator sport; it demands the messy experience of yanking
> and tinkering that comes from a limbic bond. If someone's
> relationships today bear a troubled imprint, they do so because
> an influential relationship left its mark on a child's mind. When
> a limbic connection has established a neural pattern, it takes a
> limbic connection to revise it.[98]

You and your avoidant loved one aren't going to change bad habits by
reading books, though it may help with perspective and adjusting
expectations. In the longer run, you have to practice and learn to use
more constructive patterns of attachment-related feelings and
communication to bolster your feelings that you can rely on each
other as allies in life.

If you're not ready to pursue couples or individual therapy, there is
still a lot you can do on your own. If you are lucky enough to have an
avoidant partner willing to try to accompany you on the journey, you
can embark on an joint expedition to a better future. It's even more
helpful if you have the kind of intelligent and supportive friends and
family you can enlist to the cause—by explaining to them what you
see as your issues, how you plan to change your patterns and habits to
make your lives better, and how they can help by supporting your

efforts. When those close to you—older children, parents, close friends—are aware you are trying to change your bad relationship habits, they are likely to be relieved that you are doing something about the problems they have almost certainly noticed between you.

Your friends and family, whether their attachment types are similar to yours or different, will have slightly different histories and perspectives on what is normal in terms of background and upbringing. If you can talk with them honestly about both of your needs and feelings, they can notice and point out any attitudes and expectations that seem odd or unhealthy to them but which you or your avoidant take for granted. You in turn can do the same for them, and that is just another function of friendship and personal intimacy. This exchange of views is part of what makes closeness and intimacy so valuable for personal growth, emotional health, and self-actualization. It's also a major factor in group therapy, as well as specialized support groups, since people dealing with similar problems can be examples to others, with helpful advice, encouragement, sympathy, and understanding. Troubled couples who do their best to hide their difficulties to "keep up appearances" are usually not fooling anyone close to them, and forgo the perspective and support others would give them.

Dr. Gottman (as interpreted by Dr. Nathan Cobb) suggests troubled couples beware the hostile forms of communication he calls "The Four Horseman of the Apocalypse," which when present much of the time signal a relationship close to coming apart:

> Criticism is defined as blaming, faultfinding, or using global and negative labels to attack your partner's character. For example, "How would you know? You're never home," or "My problem with you is ...." A harsh startup often comes in the form of criticism.

> Contempt is a lack of respect for your partner's dignity, an

attitude of looking down on your partner as unworthy. Forms of contempt include name-calling, put-downs, sarcasm, cynicism, swearing at each other, rolling of the eyes, mockery or hostile humor. Contempt is demeaning and conveys not just disapproval of your partner's behavior, but disgust with who your partner is. While the other three horsemen show up in small amounts in most marriages, contempt is only found in toxic relationships. This horseman also includes belligerence, which is an aggressive and angry provocation or threat.

Defensiveness is a way of turning back a perceived attack. Someone who is defensive denies their partner's statements, refuses to admit their role in problems, avoids responsibility for how they impact their partner, or deflects their partner's complaints back onto the other person. Defensiveness is destructive because it escalates tension and creates an adversarial interaction.

Stonewalling usually occurs as a result of escalating criticism, contempt and defensiveness as emotional overload becomes intense. Spouses who stonewall stubbornly refuse to give any verbal or nonverbal feedback that they are listening or attending to what their partner is saying. Often they just get up and leave the room. It's like talking to a stone wall. Stonewalling is best seen as a containment strategy that spouses use to avoid further escalation of the conflict. The problem is that the stonewaller does not just avoid the fight, but avoids his spouse and the relationship as well. According to John Gottman's research, 85% of stonewallers are men.[99]

When relationship conflicts grow heated, every attachment type exhibits a strong physiological stress reaction—which over a long term can damage health and longevity. Avoidants, especially the Dismissive type, may suppress negative feelings and deny an argument is upsetting them, but this apparent coolness is deceptive—

they are typically just as physiologically stressed. The most common pattern has an already-frustrated wife (possibly anxious-preoccupied *type,* but certainly inhabiting the anxious-preoccupied *style* after many previous incidents with her avoidant husband) starting a conversation with an attack (a "harsh startup") like, "Why haven't you started cleaning out the garage like you said you would?" This sets the negative tone for the fight that follows as the avoidant husband tries to defend himself and withdraws.

John Gottman has a vivid word for this physiological "fight-or-flight" reaction. He calls it "flooding." Flooding occurs when you and your spouse get into hostile arguments where the Four Horseman (criticism, contempt, defensiveness, and stonewalling) are allowed free reign in your relationship.

Physical signs of flooding include rapid heart rate (above 100BPM), high blood pressure, sweating, and the overwhelming urge to leave or to say something hurtful. When we become flooded, we operate mainly from a self-preservation mindset. We seek mainly to protect ourselves from the turmoil of an escalating argument, either by becoming aggressive (verbally or physically) or by trying to get away.

In distressed marriages, we commonly find habitual harsh startups by the wife combined with frequent flooding and subsequent stonewalling by the husband. This common pattern leads to a vicious communication cycle where one partner repeatedly complains, nags, criticizes and blames her spouse, while the other person repeatedly avoids, withdraws, stonewalls, or dismisses his partner. The withdrawn spouse might initially respond by counterattacking or by being defensive but eventually he switches to withdrawal in order to avoid being overwhelmed.

It becomes a cycle because the more the husband withdraws

and avoids his wife, the more frustrated and resentful she becomes. Eventually the resentment comes out as criticism and blame, which leaves her husband feeling unappreciated and overwhelmed, and so he avoids her more, so her resentment continues to build, and on it goes. Sometimes the pattern is reversed and it is the wife who withdraws and the husband who pursues.[100]

These bad habits of attack and counter-attack are very hard to get away from. Here's a list of areas to change to try to break out of the cycle:

- When you raise an issue, approach your spouse softly, respectfully. Let your choice of words be guided by an attitude of friendship and respect. Remember that this is your life partner. Think about the things you love and respect about this person. If you habitually treated a friend of yours in a mean-spirited or aggressive way how long would that person stay your friend?

- Let your partner influence you. Learn to open space for your spouse's ideas, feelings and perspectives to arise as real and valid. Try to be responsive to your partner's requests. Adopt the policy of never saying "no", outright, to your partner's needs. If you can't accomodate a request, then negotiate alternatives or other options.

- Act with positive intentions to create understanding, to show respect, and to find win-win solutions, instead of acting on your immediate, negative intentions and fears. Use your positive intentions to make and receive repair attempts.

- Learn how to self-soothe and soothe your partner through appropriate time-outs and self-reflection. Sometimes this is a necessary step in order to re-align your intentions with positive goals and to calm down enough to think about what the real issues are for you.

- Pinpoint the real issues that fuel the conflict. These are underlying needs, dreams and goals and sometimes the fears related to your needs, dreams and goals. Don't get sidetracked by arguing about details such as what your spouse said three months ago. If you are not sure what your spouse's underlying issue is, ask. Be curious. Not recognizing these underlying issues will often keep couples stuck in gridlock.

- Learn the art of compromise. Adopt a mindset that each of you have dreams and interests that need to be honored. You can find creative win-win solutions if you stop allowing your fear to be your dominant motivator. I know what some people might be thinking: "I'm not afraid. I'm just mad." But if you really stop and think about it, fear is usually at the root of what keeps people from moving out of their polarized positions—fear of losing face, fear of losing self, fear of being used, fear of getting hurt, etc.

- Learn to accept your differences and not be threatened by them. A good deal of your conflicts may arise because of how you view your differences. Conflicts rooted in personality and life experiences are not likely to go away anytime soon. It is best to learn to accept each other and focus on positives and strengths than to be preoccupied over annoying habits or dissimilar interests.

- Make requests instead of demands. Requests are respectful and open the floor for discussion. Demands will usually just intensify a power struggle.

- Begin to recognize the vicious cycle that you both co-create and take ownership of your part in that cycle. Change the cycle by interrupting it, that is, by not giving your usual response, or by stepping back and doing something different.[101]

Assuming you've worked through the couples communications issues and established a more peaceful style of interacting, what can an avoidant do to become more comfortable with intimacy? While I'm sure a good attachment-oriented therapist would be best, many cannot afford the time and money, or live too far away from anyone good. First, if you have convinced your avoidant to learn about his attachment style, there is more reading to gain further insight—see the list at the end of this chapter.

If you hang out with therapists for awhile, you'll hear about *reparenting*. This is a therapeutic technique where the therapist attempts to act as the might-have-been, better parent to the patient whose real parent left them with attachment issues; by being appropriately sensitive and supportive, the therapist can help the patient gain more attachment security. While this sounds a little New Age-y for my tastes, the overall concept is not bad. It may help to *reparent yourself*—imagine you are talking to yourself as a child who has been hurt by lack of attention or response from caregivers, and imagine yourself giving yourself the care and loving attention you deserved. As silly as this sounds to the typical Dismissive, practicing this self-support a few minutes at a time, every day for a period of time, will probably help open up a little window of improving security and insight.

And taking the time to talk over how you feel—how you *really* feel, not your idea of how you're *supposed* to feel—with your partner can help. You might even schedule a regular time—the half-hour after dinner, for example—to say only kind things to each other and be honest about your feelings, which if you are avoidant is going to be hard, but the more you do it, the easier it will get.

See Further Reading for some books that might help anyone work on their own attachment issues.

Chapter 35

Teaching Avoidants to Use Empathy

Mildly narcissistic people share a characteristic with the avoidant—limited use of empathy. Insecurity makes Avoidants more self-centered than the secure type, but they are perfectly capable of empathizing with others if they make an effort. Discussing with your Avoidant the importance of making the effort may well pay off with more sympathy and understanding; the Avoidant may be able to consciously sympathize with you and get in the habit of doing so more often if he is made aware of how helpful that is to your relationship.

This idea is supported by an article in *The Atlantic* by Olga Khazan, discussing a study which showed people with high narcissism (which many psychologists think is an extreme form of avoidance) could be persuaded to exercise their (usually less active) empathetic abilities when directed.

Only the most malignant narcissists are incapable of imagining the feelings of others; but the everyday narcissist's skill in that area is seldom used because they are always focused on what they need, ego support. When researchers asked them to put themselves in another's place, they were able to do so. This implies consistent signals rewarding displays of empathy might help the narcissist (and the avoidant) do better at acting on the feelings of others.

> Love is great, but it's actually empathy that makes the world go 'round. Understanding other peoples' viewpoints is so essential to human functioning that psychologists sometimes refer to

empathy as "social glue, binding people together and creating harmonious relationships."

Narcissists tend to lack this ability. Think of the charismatic co-worker who refuses to cover for a colleague who's been in a car accident. Or the affable friend who nonetheless seems to delight in back-stabbing.

These types of individuals are what's known as "sub-clinical" narcissists—the everyday egoists who, though they may not merit psychiatric attention, don't make very good friends or lovers.

"If people are in a romantic relationship with a narcissist, they tend to cheat on their partners and their relationships break up sooner and end quite messily," Erica Hepper, a psychologist at the University of Surrey in the U.K., told me. "They tend to be more deviant academically. They take credit for other peoples' work."

Psychologists have long thought that narcissists were largely incorrigible—that there was nothing we could do to help them be more empathetic. But for a new study in the Personality and Social Psychology Bulletin, Hepper discovered a way to measurably help narcissists feel the pain of others....

"I think what's going on here is that people who are low on narcissism are already responding to people—telling them what to do it isn't going to increase their empathy any further," Hepper said. "But the higher on narcissism you get, the less empathy [you feel]. By instructing them to think about it, it activates this empathic response that was previously much weaker."

And the narcissists weren't just faking it. In a third experiment,

Hepper showed that extreme narcissists had lower-than-average heart rates when listening to a recording of a woman in distress. (That is, "Their lack of empathy is more than skin-deep," Hepper writes.) But if they were told to take the woman's perspective, their heart rates leapt back up to a normal level.[102]

Chapter 36

Calming the Anxious-Preoccupied

A good example of the problems the Anxious-Preoccupied have in finding a good long-term partner:

> A good friend, "Jason," had gone out with "Jane" briefly, then decided there was no future to the relationship and told Jane they should just be friends ("friend-zoning," as the kids say.) Jane seemed to accept that, but continued to think of Jason as a Significant Other. Jason is a Secure, while Jane (as will become clear) is Anxious-Preoccupied.

> Months later, Jason had what amounts to a stroke and was in the hospital and rehab for months. Friends, including Jane (who normally lives hundreds of miles away), rallied around and supported Jason with visits and messages. Jason, of course, was in no shape to respond, which everyone understood.

> Then Jason returned to work, though lingering brain damage was limiting his abilities and stamina. Sometimes he responded to text messages, but usually not. He could walk only limited distances and tired easily, going to bed at 8 PM after exhausting days trying to keep up with his job. He was stubborn and independent and wanted to do everything himself. He had no energy or time for socializing.

> A few of his friends got him out to a small birthday dinner and posted a picture of the group on Facebook. That and a failure to respond to texts set off Jane, who had a meltdown on Facebook

and defriended people involved, telling everyone that Jason was obviously recovered, doing fine, and seeing someone else and intentionally lying about it.

The moral of the story: if you're Anxious-Preoccupied, your insecurities will build in the absence of reassurance, and you'll do great damage to your social ties by acting clingy, possessive, and jealous. The controlling nature of the neediness shown scares away potential partners who don't want constant drama in their relationships, and the anxious-preoccupied's fear of abandonment becomes a self-fulfilling prophecy.

From chapter 7, "Type: Anxious-Preoccupied":

> The key to happier relationships for the anxious-preoccupied is working toward an inner feeling of security and independence. This is easier when a Secure partner is present—the reliability of the partner's signalling and response reassures, letting inner security grow. But even the single Preoccupied can take a clue from their type label—they are preoccupied with the idea of a relationship. Getting involved with absorbing activities and friendships with others can take their mind off the problem of partner relationships. And self-coaching can help—replacing inner dialog about failings and worries about what others think of you with reassuring self-talk can help prevent overly-clingy and paranoid behavior that drives away significant others. Build confidence in yourself and your value by accomplishing real tasks, and try harder to see things from others' point of view before acting on fears and anger about how they treat you. Soothe your own worries before they trouble others, and have more faith in their goodwill before you assume the worst.

Part Six

When Nothing Changes

Chapter 37

Bad Relationships Harm Your Health

So what happens when you've done everything you can to improve your relationship, but you're still unhappy and trapped in a frustrating cycle of contempt and anger? Every year that you continue on this path hurts both of you—not just psychologically, but physically. While supportive partners are good for your health and help you live longer, people trapped in hostile relationships are under constant physiological stress and more likely to die.

A study written up in *Science Daily* demonstrates the heart health benefits for married couples, especially in their 50s. It is even more advantageous to be *happily* married, though this study doesn't distinguish:

> In particular, married people were 5 percent less likely to have any vascular disease compared with singles. They also had 8 percent, 9 percent and 19 percent lower odds of abdominal aortic aneurysm, cerebrovascular disease and peripheral arterial disease, respectively. The odds of coronary disease were lower in married subjects compared with those who were widowed and divorced, but this was not statistically significant when compared to single subjects, which were used as the reference group for comparison.

> On the other hand, being divorced or widowed was associated with a greater likelihood of vascular disease compared with being single or married. After multivariable adjustment, widowers had 3 percent higher odds of any vascular disease

and 7 percent higher odds of coronary artery disease. Divorce was linked with a higher likelihood of any vascular disease, abdominal aortic aneurysm, coronary artery disease and cerebrovascular disease.[103]

But when you look inside the group of married people, you discover unhappily married people have a greater risk of death, especially the men:

Results: Frequent worries/demands from partner or children were associated with 50–100% increased mortality risk. Frequent conflicts with any type of social relation were associated with 2–3 times increased mortality risk. Interaction between labour force participation and worries/demands (462 additional cases per 100 000 person-years, p=0.05) and conflicts with partner (830 additional cases per 100 000 person-years, p<0.01) was suggested. Being male and experiencing frequent worries/demands from partner produced 135 extra cases per 100 000 person-years, p=0.05 due to interaction.

Conclusions: Stressful social relations are associated with increased mortality risk among middle-aged men and women for a variety of different social roles. Those outside the labour force and men seem especially vulnerable to exposure.[104]

From *The Atlantic*, an article about the same study showing relationship conflict can be surprisingly deadly, comparing it with alternative of social isolation. The study adjusted for all the usual health risk factors but found that even for people who seemed equally healthy, conflict with people near them, especially spouses, greatly increased the risk of death:

"In your everyday life, do you experience conflicts with any of the following people?

Partner
Children
Other family
Friends
Neighbors"

A Danish health survey asked almost 10,000 people between ages 36 and 52 to answer, "always," "often," "sometimes," "seldom," or "never" for their applicable relationships.

Eleven years later, 422 of them were no longer living. That's a typical number. What's compelling, Rikke Lund and her colleagues at University of Copenhagen say, is that the people who answered "always" or "often" in any of these cases were two to three times more likely to be among the dead. (And the deaths were from standard causes: cancer, heart disease, alcohol-related liver disease, etc.—not murder. Were you thinking murder?)

The stress of constant conflict degrades health and eventually kills, it seems. But being isolated was not great, either:

In isolation, most of us wither psychologically and crumble physically. In 1979, a California epidemiological study showed that the risk of death during a given period among people with the fewest social ties was more than twice as high as in those with the most. Some experts have suggested that isolation, perceived or objective, should be commonly considered alongside things like obesity as a serious health hazard. One study found social isolation was as strong of a predictor of mortality as smoking. People with heart disease are 2.4 times more likely to die of it if they are socially isolated. We could go on and on with these decades of pro-social correlations.

So the point here is relationships are like almonds. We know that if you eat almonds, you increase your odds of living longer —unless you hate almonds so much that eating them sends you into a rage, raising your blood pressure, and you eat them every day until at some point the hypertension eventually causes a stroke. Yes, just like almonds. The objective nature of what's said or done between people converges with our personalities to create perceptions of that relationship, and that's what matters and (seems to) significantly influence our bodies. "Certain personality traits may promote the reporting of any social relation as stressful," the researchers write, "and therefore strong correlations between measures of stressful social relations would be expected."

Men did seem more physically vulnerable to worries and demands from their partner than did women, which is in keeping with a scientific understanding of men's health as especially relationship-dependent. Men release more cortisol in response to stress than women do, and marriage has proven more beneficial to men's health than to women's. And it was Harry Nilsson, not Mariah Carey, who was first moved to popularize Badfinger's "Without You" in 1971 by really drawing out the emotive i in the line, "I can't liiive if living is without you."[105]

An unhappy or stressful relationship may be worse than living alone. A study from University of Wisconsin researchers demonstrates a link between marital discord and a tendency toward depression, as the burnt-out stress system is also less activated by positive thoughts and experiences:

Marital stress may make people more vulnerable to depression, according to a recent study. The long-term study shows that people who experience chronic marital stress are less able to savor positive experiences, a hallmark of depression. They are also more likely to report other depressive symptoms. Married people are, in general, happier and healthier than single people, according to numerous studies. But marriage can also be one of the most significant sources of long-lasting social stress.[106]

Which tells us what we already knew: having as your closest partner someone who constantly stresses you out is very bad for you, while the right sort of partner reduces your stress level and increases happiness.

What does this mean for you? If you've tried everything to improve your relationship and nothing has really changed; if you feel like going to work is an escape from the stress of your home life; if you feel stressed because your partner undermines you more often than he or she supports you; you are better off leaving the relationship. And if you have children, consider how healthy it is for them to learn the model of family life they see every day. They may be better off as well.

Chapter 38

Economics of Divorce

So you're considering divorce after doing everything you can to improve your unhappy marriage. Unfortunately, it will cost you a lot in both time and money, and increase your stress level before you see any relief.

Reason Magazine writes about about Divorce Corp, a book and movie about the divorce industry and its unnecessarily expensive and complicated procedures. Reform is badly needed—one of the reasons for the declining marriage rate is the spreading knowledge that a divorce can bankrupt both parties and ruin their lives. Why take a chance on a binding contract that often costs $25-50,000 to get out of? And it's not necessary; there's no reason why all marriages have to be dissolved by a complex court proceeding. It might be cynical to note that streamlining costly and slow procedures is very difficult when state legislators are primarily lawyers and lawyers are the main beneficiaries of a complex and costly process.

> "To get divorced, you can't just simply fill out a form that says 'I'm divorced.' You have to go to court and a judge has to approve the divorce," says Divorce Corp's Joe Sorge. "Breaking up is traumatic on its own, nevermind having to go to court and appear before a judge."

> Sorge argues that because the legal code to get a divorce is so complex, nearly all respective parties have to hire expensive lawyers and pay legal fees that make the average non-contested divorce cost between $10,000 and $20,000. A contested divorce

can run well over $50,000.

"It's the fourth most common cause of bankruptcy in the United States," says Sorge.[107]

Economists talk about the concept of *sunk costs*—meaning the investment you already have in a situation, which tends to mentally block you from cutting your losses and moving on. The Freakonomics guys have written about this in the context of considering divorce in their book *Think Like a Freak: The Authors of Freakonomics Offer to Retrain Your Brain*. Here's a condensed list of decision factors:

Three primary forces bias us against quitting:

1. A lifetime of being told that quitting is a sign of failure.

2. The notion of sunk costs. As obvious as it sounds, we fail to recognize that previous investment does not justify future investment. I hear this a lot from readers who are thinking about ending their relationships. It's most prevalent when a couple's been together a really long time.

3. The failure to identify opportunity cost. When we're thinking of getting out of a relationship, we have a strong tendency to say to ourselves, "What if I never find someone else?" Instead, we should be asking ourselves what we're missing out on. Staying in a bad relationship may mean missing out on a great one.

The Formula for Knowing When to Quit:

Quit when opportunity cost outweighs sunk cost. If OC > SC, then break up. If there's the real potential for something better out there—a relationship you could happily sustain for 50 years, then what you've got invested in your current unsatisfactory relationship is immaterial.

This is not to suggest that you should end a satisfying and rewarding relationship. But if you're not satisfied in your relationship, there's a good chance that quitting it will make you happier and open you up to something better.[108]

In the US, many people now route around costly, slow, public, and adversarial probate courts (which divide up estates on death) by using trust structures; the "Living Trust" (revocable personal trust) holds your assets and on death they are directed to beneficiaries by a trustee without court filings, delays, publicity, battling lawyers, or expense. Something similar, where couples agree on a dissolution trust going in with a trusted (and cheaper) mediator to execute the agreement, might get rid of most divorce costs for most people.

Chapter 39

Moneyball: Finding a New Partner

So you've given up on your marriage or relationship with your avoidant partner. How do you find a new partner, now that you're older and wiser? For one thing, if you haven't already, read my book on the subject: *Bad Boyfriends: Using Attachment Theory to Avoid Mr. (or Ms.) Wrong and Make You a Better Partner.*

And don't get distracted by superficial factors and fixate on sexiness or apparent success in choosing a new partner; don't neglect the solid and unflashy sorts who may not look very exciting, but have the loyalty and ability to keep you interested and happy over the very long run.

One of my many hats is investor/economist, so the story "The Science of Settling: Calculate Your Mate With Moneyball" at NPR, about applying economic thinking to mate-seeking, got my attention:

> ... [T]here's another type of virtual eyewear that many of us spend even more time donning—one that has the opposite effect of beer goggles. Call them "expectancy spectacles" if you'd like, because wearing them causes us to raise our standards and expectations, often unrealistically, of everything from potential mates to job prospects.

> The primary culprit behind this altered vision is not booze, but a potent concoction of Hollywood movies, social conditioning and wishful thinking. And fortunately, there are a few scientists on the case.

One is Ty Tashiro, a psychologist specializing in romantic relationships who writes for Discovery Fit and Health. His recent book, *The Science of Happily Ever After*, explores what "advances in relationship science" can teach us about the partners we choose. Almost 9 in 10 Americans believe they have a soul mate, says Tashiro, but only 3 in 10 find enduring partnerships that do not end in divorce, separation or chronic unhappiness. Clearly something is going wrong—and it starts with our expectations.

That's because in real life the pool of potential partners looks rather different from the cast of The Bachelorette—something Tashiro hopes to address by putting some cold figures to the mating game, employing an approach similar to the one used by scientists who calculate the chances of life on other planets.

For example, say a bachelorette enters a room of 100 male bachelors who represent the broader U.S population. If she prefers a partner who's tall (at least 6 feet), then her pool of possible prospects immediately shrinks to 20. If she would like him to be fairly attractive and earn a comfortable income (over $87,000 annually), then she's down to a single prospect out of 100.

If you choose to specify further traits, such as kindness, intelligence or a particular religious or political affiliation, well, let's just say we're going to need a much bigger room. And then, of course, there's the small matter of whether he actually likes you back.

Such long odds are the product of misplaced priorities, says Tashiro, but it's not strictly our fault. Our mate preferences have been shaped by natural selection's obsession with physical attractiveness and resources as well as the messages our friends, families and favorite shows transmit about sweethearts and soul mates. And it is at the start of relationships, when we need to make smart, long-term decisions, that we are least likely to do so because we're in the throes of lust, passion and romance.

Or, as Tashiro puts it, returning to our alcohol analogy: "It would seem wise to hand off the keys to someone with more lucidity until your better sensibilities return."

Which is why Tashiro advocates a new approach to dating, one that is not so much about lowering standards as giving yourself better ones. Call it "Moneyballing" relationships (Tashiro does); it's all about finding undervalued traits and assets in the dating market. And, just like with baseball, it starts with trying to ignore the superficial indices of value—attractiveness, wealth— in favor of hidden attributes with a stronger correlation to long-term relationship success.

Citing research that finds no reliable link between income level or physical attractiveness and relationship satisfaction, Tashiro steers his readers toward traits such as agreeableness. With married couples, he points out, "liking declines at a rate of 3 percent a year, whereas lust declines at a rate of 8 percent per year," so the smarter, long-term investment is finding someone you genuinely like. Plus, he adds, studies also suggest that agreeable partners are in fact "better in bed" and less likely to cheat over the long haul.[109]

Being confused about what you are looking for in a mate is epidemic —part of the cost of freedom to choose yourself (instead of having parents arranging your marriage for you) is valuing the wrong things and being unrealistic about what your partner should be like. Programmed by the Fairy Tale model ("(s)he should be just perfect and make me happy!") most young people don't have the sense to look beyond the superficial unless they are lucky enough to accidentally come into close contact with a person who they can love unconditionally. Much more likely, they will dismiss many good long-term partner candidates for failing to be exactly as expected— not tall enough, not rich enough, not goodlooking enough... "I deserve better!"

The "Moneyball" reference is to the problem of assembling the best baseball team for the least money. The obvious stars are pursued by many teams and their salaries bid up; because of the overvaluation of the very best players, one manager discovered he could assemble a great team at a lower cost by focusing on the less obvious players, who might be very good at one or two things which went unrecognized.

In the mate-seeking problem, the analogous strategy is to not be distracted by good looks or superficial factors like current wealth, height, or sexiness. The people who have all those things are in great demand, know it, and are less likely to pick you for partnership. Meanwhile, the shy, short guy with the entrepreneurial spirit and drive will someday be wealthy, the plain and unfashionably dressed girl with smarts may blossom into a glamourous woman as she makes it out in the world and has the time and money to work on appearance.

When you are thinking long-term, think like an investor—go after the future great partner, not the ones who satisfy all your shallow "must haves" right now. Love and commitment make high achievers out of good partners and create that successful life the Fairy Tale talks about; but it doesn't just happen, you have to work for it and believe in your partner. Look for someone you can trust and believe in.

Chapter 40

Attachment Types in the Dating Pool

Estimates vary, but a good guess is that 50% of the population starts adulthood secure, while 20% are anxious-preoccupied, 25% are dismissive-avoidant, and 5% are fearful-avoidant. But as time goes by and the secure are more likely to get into and stay in long-term relationships, the proportions of the types seen in the dating pool change—the secure become scarce, and the dismissive-avoidant, who begin and end relationships quickly, become the most likely type you will encounter.

The following graph shows a simulation of the type frequency in the dating population over time given the different expected rates of coupling and breakup for each type:

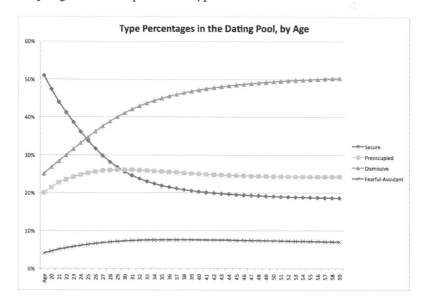

Graph Showing Types Over Time[110]

> This graph is based on a simplified simulation of the dating
> pool by age, showing the percentage of each type in the
> shrinking dating pool. Secures appear dominant early in the
> dating pool at about 50%, but over time their prevalence
> declines to around 20%. Notice how the Dismissive-Avoidant
> start off as the second most prevalent attachment type at 25%,
> but over time become the predominant type at 50% of the far
> smaller dating population—this is not because they don't start
> relationships, but that they tend to exit them quickly. The
> proportion of Preoccupied and Fearful-Avoidant increases
> somewhat as well. The age scale assumes everyone starts
> looking for a partner at 20, so subpopulations which start later
> (academics, for example) would be shifted by a few years. Since
> both starting parameters and the simulation are simplified,
> these numbers are only suggestive.

The shrinkage of the dating pool with time and its later domination
by less secure types means the older you are, the more cautious you
should be, because it is much more likely that those in the dating pool
in later years have a problematic attachment type, or even worse
problems keeping them from sustaining good relationships. Of
course there are always new entries to the dating pool who have been
released from good relationships by their partner's death or
unfortunate circumstances; but those past 40 who have never been
able to get and keep a good relationship going, likely never will—
unless of course they have realized they need to change and work
hard on themselves.

Further Reading

General Books on Attachment

Kinnison, Jeb. *Bad Boyfriends: Using Attachment Theory to Avoid Mr. (or Ms.) Wrong and Make You a Better Partner.* My first book on attachment theory and types, aimed at assisting those looking for a mate. Has more on dating, recognizing the types, and avoiding the dangerous and unsupportive candidates.

Lewis, Thomas; Amini, Fari; and Lannon, Richard. *A General Theory of Love.* New York: Vintage Books, 2001. This book is a synthesis of the scientific work in the study of attachment and love. It's moving and accessible, and brings together topics of neuroscience and psychology with an entertaining literary sensibility.

Karen, Robert. *Becoming Attached: First Relationships and How They Shape Our Capacity to Love.* New York: Oxford University Press, 1998. If you're interested in a detailed look at the effects of upbringing on child and adult attachment, this is the one to read.

Levine, Amir, and Heller, Rachel. *Attached: The New Science of Adult Attachment and How It Can Help You Find—and Keep—Love.* New York: Jeremy P. Tarcher, 2010. Popular book with a wealth of advice and stories about how the anxious-preoccupied, especially, can change their dating strategies and behaviors.

Therapeutic Techniques

Wallin, David J. *Attachment in Psychotherapy.* New York: Guilford Press, 2007. Highly technical book for therapists and motivated others about the therapeutic process when attachment styles are the primary issues. Currently expensive.

Shaver, Philip, and Cassidy, Jude, editors. *Handbook of Attachment, Second Edition: Theory, Research, and Clinical Applications.* Guilford Press, 2008. Survey of research in the field and therapeutic techniques, primarily for professionals in the field.

Stone, Hal, and Sidra. *Embracing Our Selves: the Voice Dialogue Manual.* San Rafael, Calif.: New World Library, 1989.

Relationship and Marriage Communication

Johnson, Susan M. *Hold Me Tight: Seven Conversations for a Lifetime of Love.* New York: Little, Brown & Co., 2008. Another popular book with good advice on learning to be a better communicator and partner.

Gottman, John. *The Seven Principles for Making Marriage Work.* A great guide on how to strive for better communication and satisfaction with your partner, especially when you are insecure.

For the Anxious-Preoccupied

Becker-Phelps, Leslie. *Insecure in Love: How Anxious Attachment Can Make You Feel Jealous, Needy, and Worried and What You Can Do About It* . New Harbinger, 2014. Specific tips and self-help techniques for the anxious-preoccupied.

Acknowledgements

Thanks to my readers for continuing to educate me on the importance of attachment in their lives, especially those who shared their stories and allowed me to use them as examples.

Thanks to my volunteer editors, who have saved me from much embarrassment.

And thanks to my attached others, who keep my life centered, yet leave me time to work.

Online Resources

If you enjoyed this book and believe as I do that a better understanding of attachment types would do a lot to make most people's lives better, please help me get the word out by telling your friends about *Bad Boyfriends* (which is for everyone) and this book, *Avoidant* (which is for people already with an avoidant.) And please do me the great favor of writing a short review at Amazon, Goodreads, Barnes and Noble, or other book site. As a small publisher, we can't afford marketing campaigns or product placement payments to bookstores.

For up-to-date news on relationship topics and the author's work, please go to my web site at jebkinnison.com, and if you want to be regularly notified of updates, sign up for my mailing list there. Since online resources change frequently, I have a groomed list of better web sites there for further exploration.

If you'd like to email me directly with questions, errata, or comments, I'm at jebkinnison@gmail.com.

About the Author

I grew up in the Midwest, child of a schizophrenic father and a hardworking single mother. At 12, I was deemed brilliant but uncontrollable, and I was sent to a private psychiatric hospital, where I was grilled about my sexual fantasies (which, not surprisingly, made me acutely uncomfortable). But this experience had me spending a lot of time with psychologists and psychiatric residents, which got me interested in the topic.

I studied computer and cognitive science at MIT, and wrote programs modeling the behavior of simulated stock traders and the population dynamics of economic agents. Later I did supercomputer work at a think tank that developed parts of the early Internet (where the engineer who decided on '@' as the separator for email addresses worked down the hall.) Since then I have had several careers—real estate, financial advising, and counselling.

In attachment terms, in high school I was behind in social development (this was not surprising since my mother worked all day and my father was AWOL) and had to learn about people to catch up. So I started my 20s mildly anxious-preoccupied, had two lengthy but imperfect relationships, and finally matured into a more secure type. Now married and definitely secure.

I recently visited the Mormon genealogical web site, which shows me as a descendant of Eleanor of Aquitaine, Edward I Plantagenet (King of England!), William the Conqueror (who you might remember from such historical events as the Norman Conquest of 1066), and Rollo the Viking. It appears that my ancestors in between lost track of their money, lands, and power, so I was brought up in "reduced circumstances."

Visit my web site at JebKinnison.com for more: rail guns, Nazi scientists, the wreck of the *Edmund Fitzgerald*, the 1980s AI bubble, and current research in relationships, attachment types, diet, and health.

Notes

[1] Note this use of "avoidant" is unrelated to the DSM handbook's diagnosis of Avoidant Personality Disorder. It is handy to refer to both Fearful-Avoidants and Dismissive-Avoidants as "avoidants" to cover their common features, but they are not social phobics; they are intimacy-avoidant. See Avoidant Personality Disorder for that definition.

[2] Mikulincer, M., Shaver, P.R., & Pereg, D. (2003). Attachment theory and affect regulation: The dynamics, development, and cognitive consequences of attachment-related strategies. *Motivation and Emotion*, 27, 77–102.

[3] From http://en.wikipedia.org/wiki/Attachment_in_adults

[4] Smith, Emily Esfahani. "Masters of Love." *The Atlantic*, June 12, 2014. http://www.theatlantic.com/health/archive/2014/06/happily-ever-after/372573/.

[5] Smith, Emily Esfahani. "Masters of Love." *The Atlantic*, June 12, 2014. http://www.theatlantic.com/health/archive/2014/06/happily-ever-after/372573/.

[6] Smith, Emily Esfahani. "Masters of Love." *The Atlantic*, June 12, 2014. http://www.theatlantic.com/health/archive/2014/06/happily-ever-after/372573/.

[7] Smith, Emily Esfahani. "Masters of Love." *The Atlantic*, June 12, 2014. http://www.theatlantic.com/health/archive/2014/06/happily-ever-after/372573/.

[8] http://internal.psychology.illinois.edu/~rcfraley/
R. Chris Fraley, University of Illinois at Urbana-Champaign, Department of Psychology, 603 East Daniel Street, Champaign, IL 61820

[9] Karen, Robert. *Becoming Attached: First Relationships and How They Shape Our Capacity to Love*. New York: Oxford University Press, 1998.
p. 388

[10] Goldman, Daniel. "Emotional Intelligence," 1995 Bantam

[11] Karen, p. 364

[12] Karen, p. 372

[13] Karen, p. 382

[14] Levine, Amir, and Rachel Heller. *Attached: The New Science of Adult Attachment and How It Can Help You Find—and Keep—Love*. New York: Jeremy P. Tarcher, 2010. p. 136.

[15] Karen, p. 366

[16] Karen, p. 372

[17] Karen, p. 375

[18] Karen, p. 376

[19] Karen, p. 383

[20] Karen, p. 385

[21] Karen, p. 399

[22] Karen, p. 387

[23] Levine, Amir, and Heller, Rachel. *Attached: The New Science of Adult Attachment and How It Can Help You Find—and Keep—Love*. New York: Jeremy P. Tarcher, 2010. p. 80.

[24] Levine, Amir, and Heller, Rachel. *Attached: The New Science of Adult Attachment and How It Can Help You Find—and Keep—Love*. New York: Jeremy P. Tarcher, 2010. p. 80.

[25] Levine, Amir, and Heller, Rachel. *Attached: The New Science of Adult Attachment and How It Can Help You Find—and Keep—Love*. New York: Jeremy P. Tarcher, 2010. p. 86.

[26] "Approach-Avoidance Conflict." *Wikipedia, the Free Encyclopedia*, January 4, 2014. http://en.wikipedia.org/w/index.php?title=Approach-avoidance_conflict&oldid=589161815.

[27] Karen, p. 373

[28] Miller, Alice. *The Drama of the Gifted Child: The Search for the True Self, Revised Edition*. Basic Books, 1996.

[29] Karen, p. 365

[30] Karen, p. 383

[31] Karen, p. 384

[32] Karen, p. 399

[33] Karen, p. 387

[34] Levine and Heller, p. 117

[35] "Alexithymia" http://en.wikipedia.org/wiki/Alexithymia

[36] Mikulincer, Mario. *Attachment in Adulthood: Structure, Dynamics, and Change*. Kindle edition loc. 7383. The Guilford Press, 2007.

[37] Mikulincer, Mario. *Attachment in Adulthood: Structure, Dynamics, and Change*. Kindle edition loc. 7410. The Guilford Press, 2007.

[38] "+THOUGHTS - INCLUDING DISMISSIVE-AVOIDANT INSECURE ATTACHMENT DISORDER." *Stop the Storm*. Accessed September 23, 2014. http://stopthestorm.wordpress.com/2010/08/22/thoughts-including-dismissive-avoidant-insecure-attachment-disorder/.

[39] Vrticka, Pascal, and Patrik Vuilleumier. "Neuroscience of Human Social Interactions and Adult Attachment Style." *Frontiers in Human Neuroscience* 6 (2012): 212. doi:10.3389/fnhum.2012.00212.

[40] Mikulincer, Mario. *Attachment in Adulthood: Structure, Dynamics, and Change*. Kindle edition, loc. 8290. The Guilford Press, 2007.

[41] Mikulincer, Mario. *Attachment in Adulthood: Structure, Dynamics, and Change*. Kindle edition, loc. 8300. The Guilford Press, 2007.

[42] Mikulincer, Mario. *Attachment in Adulthood: Structure, Dynamics, and Change*. Kindle edition, loc. 8408. The Guilford Press, 2007.

[43] Mikulincer, Mario. *Attachment in Adulthood: Structure, Dynamics, and Change*. Kindle edition, loc. 8418. The Guilford Press, 2007.

[44] http://www.mdjunction.com/forums/emotional-abuse-discussions/general-support/10708676-small-ventwhen-dad-is-uncaring-and-dismissive

[45] "Emotionally Unavailable Father; The Message of Passive Abuse:: Emerging From Broken." Accessed September 21, 2014. http://emergingfrombroken.com/emotionally-unavailable-father-the-message-of-passive-abuse/.

[46] Mikulincer, Mario. *Attachment in Adulthood: Structure, Dynamics, and Change*. Kindle edition, loc. 7717. The Guilford Press, 2007.

[47] Mikulincer, Mario. *Attachment in Adulthood: Structure, Dynamics, and Change*. Kindle edition, loc. 7875. The Guilford Press, 2007.

[48] Mikulincer, Mario. *Attachment in Adulthood: Structure, Dynamics, and Change*. Kindle edition, loc. 7901. The Guilford Press, 2007.

[49] Mikulincer, Mario. *Attachment in Adulthood: Structure, Dynamics, and Change*. Kindle edition loc. 7923. The Guilford Press, 2007.

[50] Levine and Heller, p. 117

[51] Mikulincer, Mario; Shaver, Phillip. *Attachment in Adulthood: Structure, Dynamics, and Change*. The Guilford Press, 2007.

[52] Levine and Heller, p. 117

[53] Karen, Robert. *Becoming Attached: First Relationships and How They Shape Our Capacity to Love*. p. 396. New York: Oxford University Press, 1998.

[54] Karen, Robert. *Becoming Attached: First Relationships and How They Shape Our Capacity to Love*. p. 404. New York: Oxford University Press, 1998.

[55] Levine, Amir, and Rachel Heller. *Attached: The New Science of Adult Attachment and How It Can Help You Find- and Keep -Love*. p. 91. New York: Jeremy P. Tarcher, 2010.

[56] "Why Your Partner May Be Like Your Parent." Accessed September 18, 2014. http://www.psychologytoday.com/blog/tech-support/201405/why-your-partner-may-be-your-parent.

[57] Levine, Amir, and Rachel Heller. *Attached: The New Science of Adult Attachment and How It Can Help You Find- and Keep -Love*. p. 96. New York: Jeremy P. Tarcher, 2010.

[58] Mikulincer, Mario. *Attachment in Adulthood: Structure, Dynamics, and Change*. Kindle edition, loc. 7483. The Guilford Press, 2007.

[59] Mikulincer, Mario. *Attachment in Adulthood: Structure, Dynamics, and Change*. Kindle edition, loc. 7443. The Guilford Press, 2007.

[60] Mikulincer, Mario. *Attachment in Adulthood: Structure, Dynamics, and Change*. Kindle edition, loc. 8058. The Guilford Press, 2007.

[61] Paul Schrodt, Paul L. Witt, Jenna R. Shimkowski. "A Meta-Analytical Review of the Demand-Withdraw Pattern of Interaction and its Associations with Individual, Relational, and Communicative Outcomes." Communication Monographs Vol. 81, Iss. 1, 2014

[62] Mikulincer, Mario. *Attachment in Adulthood: Structure, Dynamics, and Change*. Kindle edition, loc. 7410. The Guilford Press, 2007.

[63] Mikulincer, Mario. *Attachment in Adulthood: Structure, Dynamics, and Change*. Kindle edition, loc. 7901. The Guilford Press, 2007.

[64] Mikulincer, Mario. *Attachment in Adulthood: Structure, Dynamics, and Change*. Kindle edition loc. 7920. The Guilford Press, 2007.

[65] Mikulincer, Mario. *Attachment in Adulthood: Structure, Dynamics, and Change*. Kindle edition loc. 7423. The Guilford Press, 2007.

[66] Just Four Guys blog post "Solange Knowles, Ray Rice: Compare & Contrast," http://www.justfourguys.com/solange-knowles-ray-rice-compare-contrast/

[67] Mikulincer, Mario; Shaver, Phillip. *Attachment in Adulthood: Structure, Dynamics, and Change*. The Guilford Press, 2007.

[68] Mikulincer, Mario; Shaver, Phillip. *Attachment in Adulthood: Structure, Dynamics, and Change.* The Guilford Press, 2007.

[69] Mikulincer, Mario; Shaver, Phillip. *Attachment in Adulthood: Structure, Dynamics, and Change.* The Guilford Press, 2007.

[70] Mikulincer, Mario; Shaver, Phillip. *Attachment in Adulthood: Structure, Dynamics, and Change.* The Guilford Press, 2007.

[71] Mikulincer, Mario. *Attachment in Adulthood: Structure, Dynamics, and Change.* Kindle edition, loc. 8868. The Guilford Press, 2007.

[72] Mikulincer, Mario. *Attachment in Adulthood: Structure, Dynamics, and Change.* Kindle edition, loc. 8891. The Guilford Press, 2007.

[73] Mikulincer, Mario. *Attachment in Adulthood: Structure, Dynamics, and Change.* Kindle edition, loc. 8872. The Guilford Press, 2007.

[74] Mikulincer, Mario. *Attachment in Adulthood: Structure, Dynamics, and Change.* Kindle edition, loc. 8941. The Guilford Press, 2007.

[75] Mikulincer, Mario; Shaver, Phillip. *Attachment in Adulthood: Structure, Dynamics, and Change.* The Guilford Press, 2007.

[76] Manson, Mark. "6 Healthy Relationship Habits Most People Think Are Toxic." *Mark Manson.* Accessed September 23, 2014. http://markmanson.net/6-healthy-habits/.

[77] Manson, Mark. "6 Healthy Relationship Habits Most People Think Are Toxic."

[78] Manson, Mark. "6 Healthy Relationship Habits Most People Think Are Toxic."

[79] Manson, Mark. "6 Healthy Relationship Habits Most People Think Are Toxic."

[80] "Why Women Can't Find a Good Man." Jeremy Nicholson, *Psychology Today* Blogs. Accessed September 22, 2014. http://www.psychologytoday.com/blog/the-attraction-doctor/201203/why-women-cant-find-good-man.

[81] "Why Women Can't Find a Good Man."

[82] Berg, Piet Van Den, and Tim W. Fawcett. "Evolution and Bad Boyfriends." *The New York Times*, October 11, 2013, sec. Opinion / Sunday Review. http://www.nytimes.com/2013/10/13/opinion/sunday/evolution-and-bad-boyfriends.html.

[83] Berg, Piet Van Den, and Tim W. Fawcett. "Evolution and Bad Boyfriends."

[84] Berg, Piet Van Den, and Tim W. Fawcett. "Evolution and Bad Boyfriends."

[85] "New Research: When it hurts to think we were made for each other."

University of Toronto, Rotman School of Management. http://www.rotman.utoronto.ca/Connect/MediaCentre/NewsReleases/20140722.aspx

[86] Kposowa, A. J. "Divorce and Suicide Risk." *Journal of Epidemiology and Community Health* 57, no. 12 (December 1, 2003): 993–993. doi:10.1136/jech.57.12.993.

[87] Gunther, Randi. "Why Great Husbands Are Being Abandoned." *Psychology Today* blog. Accessed September 23, 2014. http://www.psychologytoday.com/blog/rediscovering-love/201408/why-great-husbands-are-being-abandoned-0.

[88] Sapolsky, Robert M. "New Ways to Predict Which Marriages Will Succeed." *Wall Street Journal*, August 21, 2014, sec. Life and Style. http://online.wsj.com/articles/new-ways-to-predict-which-marriages-will-succeed-1408636006.

[89] Smith, Emily Esfahani. "Masters of Love." *The Atlantic*, June 12, 2014. http://www.theatlantic.com/health/archive/2014/06/happily-ever-after/372573/.

[90] Smith, Emily Esfahani. "Masters of Love."

[91] Smith, Emily Esfahani. "Masters of Love."

[92] Smith, Emily Esfahani. "Masters of Love."

[93] "About the Gottman Method - for Couples and Therapists." *The Gottman Institute*. Accessed September 23, 2014. http://www.gottman.com/about-gottman-method-couples-therapy/.

[94] Mikulincer, Mario. *Attachment in Adulthood: Structure, Dynamics, and Change*. Kindle edition, loc. 10826. The Guilford Press, 2007.

[95] Lewis, p 278

[96] Karen, p. 370

[97] Lewis, p 170

[98] Lewis, p 177

[99] Cobb, Nathan. "Communication and Conflict Resolution." Accessed September 24, 2014. http://www.nathancobb.com/communication.html.

[100] "Communication and Conflict Resolution."

[101] "Communication and Conflict Resolution."

[102] Khazan, Olga. "How to Make the Narcissist in Your Life a Little Nicer." *The Atlantic*, June 3, 2014. http://www.theatlantic.com/health/archive/2014/06/how-to-make-the-narcissist-in-your-life-a-little-nicer/372072/.

[103] "Marriage Linked to Lower Heart Risks in Study of More than 3.5 Million